Chanting

Chanting

Discovering Spirit in Sound

Robert Gass

with

Kathleen Brehony

Broadway Books
New York

BROADWAY

Broadway Books titles may be purchased for business or promotional use or for
special sales. For information, please write to: Special Markets Department,
Random House, Inc., 1540 Broadway, New York, NY 10036.

BROADWAY BOOKS and its logo, a letter B bisected on the diagonal, are
trademarks of Broadway Books, a division of Random House, Inc.

Library of Congress Cataloging-in-Publication Data
Gass, Robert, 1948–
Chanting : discovering spirit in sound / by Robert Gass
with Kathleen Brehony.—1st ed.
p.   cm.
Includes bibliographical references and index.
ISBN 0-7679-0322-6 (hc)
1. Chants.   2. Spiritual life.   I. Brehony, Kathleen A.   II. Title.
BL560.G37   1999
291.3′7—dc21   98-50760
CIP

FIRST EDITION

Designed by James Sinclair

99   00   01   02   03   10   9   8   7   6   5   4   3   2   1

for Judith

Contents

Foreword

Fifteen years ago, I began a book on chant. I met with publishers and editors in New York, but none of them believed that there was any interest outside liturgical and musicological circles in this fundamental expression of life. They thought chant was neither practical nor inspiring for the public. It was outdated and boring. Chant was an esoteric musical energy reserved for the monks, shamans, and singers in remote forests, monasteries, and music schools.

For me, however, tone and chant were the very basis of life. After two decades of visiting monasteries in Greece, Egypt, Russia, and France, as well as ashrams in India and temples in Japan, Korea, China, and Tibet, I was certain that there was far more to these devoted utterances than just singing. Chant is the music of the cosmic spheres and the natural expression of our own consciousness. Chant is not an obscure musical ritual—it is an important tool used by people everywhere to heal their bodies, quiet their minds, and bring the sacred into their lives.

The past decade has witnessed Gregorian chant becoming a bestselling phenomenon in Europe and America. Robert Gass's recordings of chant have inspired hundreds of thousands of listeners and helped revive the power of the repeated musical prayer.

Why? Because chant unifies. It brings people together in thought, intention, knowledge, and love. Chant is more than a repetitious song—it is an extraordinary way to integrate breath, heartbeat, emotion, and purpose. Chant reaches across spiritual, political, and social boundaries. The instant we open our mouths, the sound of chant vibrates through our bodies, bringing increased bloodflow to the head, balancing brainwaves, and inspiring the singer as well as the listener. It has long served to bring spiritual communities together, to bring workers into synchronized physical movement, and to cheer football players into action.

This long overdue and important book helps us to see how we can use our voices, spirits, and bodies to foster greater harmony in our communities and families. *Chanting: Discovering Spirit in Sound* brings to life a remarkable world of devotional expression. The simple and practical exercises included here, along with the imaginative descriptions of chant as a living presence of faith, hope, and joy, give us the keys to unlock our bodies, minds, and hearts.

Let us all take note of the variety of great music that resonates throughout our world and not forget to enchant our lives with it every day. It can release stress, connect us with the Divine, and help us bring peace to our being and to our world.

—Don Campbell

Acknowledgments

This book was a collective effort of many people inspired by the vision of a book bringing the joy and spirit of chanting to the world.

To Kathy Brehony, my coauthor, my deepest and heartfelt thanks. Without her immense dedication and hard work, her brilliant research and written contributions, this book would never have happened.

My love and gratitude to my wife, Judith, wise woman and artist of life, for her collaboration and support in writing this book, and for our thirty-year journey of deepening in love.

Thanks to Lisa Ross, whose creative spark first conceived this book on chant. Acknowledgment also goes to Chaula Hopefisher for her initial help in giving it form. Lauren Marino and Ann Campbell at Broadway Books recognized the importance of this project and have supported it every step of the way.

Chant leaders, sound healers, shamans, monks, priests, rabbis, chanters, wisdom keepers, and scholars from many traditions and disciplines gave generously of their experience and expertise. Their stories and knowledge gifted our project wih spirit, depth, and substance:

Elena Abila, Swami Akandananda, Elias Amidon, Margot Anand, Madame Andrews, Ysaye Barnwell, Isabella Bates, Joan Borysenko, George Brandon, Brooke Medicine Eagle, Don

Campbell, Deepak Chopra, Ron Claman and Toby Jacobson, Elizabeth Cogburn, Pat Moffitt Cook, Tenzin Dhargye, Vickie Dodd, Rabbi Tirzah Firestone, Steven and Meredith Foster, Shaykh Robert Ragip Frager, David Friedman, Neil Friedman, Kay Gardner, Judith Gass, Jonathan Goldman, Geoffrey Gordon, Joan Halifax, Prajna Hallstrom, Michael Harrison, Thomas and Priya Huffman, David Hykes, Chris Johnston, Chaitanya Kabir, Jack Kessler, Saadi Neil Douglas Klotz, Krishnabai, David LaChapelle, Deforia Lane, Robert Lawlor, Joshua Leeds, Allaudin Mathieu, Charlotte Miller, Ron Minson, Oscar Miro-Quesada, Daniel Abd al-Hayy Moore, Onye Onyemaechi, Russill Paul, Richard Perl, Roger Peyton, Brother Richard of Weston Priory, Dinabandu Patton Sarley, Rabbi Zalman Schachter-Shalomi, Molly Scott, Bernie Siegel, Ranjie Singh, Cynthia Snodgrass, Lama Surya Das, Luisah Teish, Father Theophane, Karolyn van Putten, Jeff Volk, Nuttarote Wangwingyoo, Joyce Wells, Michael Ziegler, and Zuleika.

I would especially like to thank my readers—those people who reviewed chapters for flow and accuracy: George Brandon, Don Campbell, Shaykh Robert Ragip Frager, Judith Gass, Leila Gass, Prajna Hallstrom, Oscar Miro-Quesada, John Makransky, Daniel Abd al-Hayy Moore, and Rabbi Zalman Schachter-Shalomi.

Thanks also to Jean Houston, Jon Kabat-Zinn, Eric and Nina Utne, and Robert Welsch.

A joyful appreciation to the many singers in On Wings of Song for our twenty years of creating together such beautiful music of the Spirit.

My gratitude to Bill Horwedel, Tim Shove, and all the folks at Spring Hill Music for their support.

Lastly, I want to thank my family and friends for illuminating my life with love and happiness.

Chanting

Chapter One

A Journey: From Bach to Rock to Chant

"Music is well said to be the speech of angels."
—Thomas Carlyle

At the age of eighty-five, my grandmother Miriam was still wearing miniskirts and teaching folk dancing on the boardwalk at Coney Island. She had studied yoga, and whenever I came to visit she immediately demonstrated her continued splendid health by standing on her head in her miniskirt. I once asked Nana, who had outlived four husbands, the secret of her vitality. She confided that she had taught herself meditation and had been practicing for over ten years. I was intrigued, given my own many years as a meditator, and asked her, "Nana, what do you do when you meditate?"

"I read in a book on yoga that you're supposed to take an Indian word and repeat it over and over again," she answered. "So I picked my own Indian word, and I've been chanting my mantra (she pronounced it *man*-tra in her thick Brooklynese accent) every day all these years."

Growing more curious by the moment, I asked, "Nana, what is

the word you use?" Proudly she answered, "Cheyenne, Cheyenne, Cheyenne."

Not knowing the difference, my dear Nana had chosen the name of a Native American tribe instead of one of the sacred Sanskrit syllables from India that are usually used in meditation. But as she talked about her experiences of chanting her sacred "man-tra" over ten years, I was struck by the obvious benefits to her life and being—physically, emotionally, and spiritually.

And so it is with profound respect for the power of chant, as well as a smile in the face of the mystery that is life, that I begin this book.

A Personal Path

Many people I know speak of the deep connection they felt to Spirit when they were children. I'm not sure that was true for me. I grew up in a liberal Jewish family with a strong emphasis on values, but there seemed to be about as much living Spirit in my synagogue as in an average shopping mall. As a child, my only Gods played for the Boston Red Sox, and the chief deity I worshiped was leftfielder Ted Williams. I came out of childhood and many years of religious-based education a proud agnostic.

Yet one of my earliest memories is of sitting at the old ebony piano in my grandparents' house on Sunday afternoons, turning dog-eared yellow pages of musical notes, pretending to read, my hands romping freely across the keys. I would lose track of time, journeying far from their musty house with its faded memories and bric-a-brac of another era, and entering another world, a magical place filled with colors and energy.

As I grew up, the piano became my playmate in times of happiness and, later, my refuge when, at eleven years old, a great darkness settled over our home as my mother lay upstairs painfully dying of cancer. Swaying on the piano bench, my hands now more masterfully working the aging ivories, I felt and expressed things through music that were too hard to express in words. Again, I was transported into another realm where colors were brighter, where pulses of energy created a continually changing tapestry of patterns, being woven and rewoven; a realm where I was no longer desperately alone, and where I felt alive and connected to something larger than myself.

Some years later as a graduating high-school senior, I was asked to pick a quote to accompany my yearbook picture. Though I was still an avowed unbeliever with no conscious relationship to religion or Spirit, I chose the quote, "Music is well said to be the speech of angels." Looking back, I see that even without a religious context or any concept of spirituality, I intimately knew God through music.

Recognizing my passion and my gift, my parents had supported me in intensive study of keyboard, music theory, and composition from the age of six. My piano teachers saw in me the possibility of realizing their own unfulfilled ambitions and tried to push me toward competitions and concert halls. But although I loved the classics, I had already begun to discover the power of simple music to move groups of people. Long before I encountered chant, there was musical comedy, and whenever there was a piano for me to play, people would gather round and we would sing songs from *West Side Story* and *My Fair Lady*. I also began playing my accordion in "hootenannies"—jam sessions with people of all musical abilities, singing and playing simple folk songs. Long-repeating choruses were a specialty, because everyone could forget about the words and get lost in the music.

My classical training at the New England Conservatory, Tanglewood, and Harvard exposed me to music that was increasingly complex and abstract. In fact, my fellow composers liked to intimate that if too many people "understood" or liked your music, it meant that you had probably "sold out." Although I was engaged by the intellectual challenge, I never fully embraced that path. I wanted to make music that was accessible, that was from the heart—music through which others could express their own songs and dreams.

Harvard in the late sixties was in creative ferment, and like others of my generation, I was swept away in a tidal wave of passion and politics. Music was married to causes, and I learned to intentionally use song to shift the consciousness of people gathered at political rallies and protests. Thousands of us, chanting as we marched or swaying hand-in-hand, experienced a form of communion. We were a tribe, joined in common cause, and music helped hold us together.

In 1967, I became a professional rock musician. Rock concerts in those days were tribal events—true Dionysian rituals. One night it was the Fillmore East in New York City, the next it was the banks of the Charles River in Cambridge, or a nameless club in D.C. Jimmy, our drummer, laid down a heavy beat as the lead guitar screamed a series of crashing power chords. The crowd jumped to its feet as it received the pulse of energy emanating from the stage. As the music took off, I began to experience a familiar cycle. Throbbing from the stage, the music aroused the energy of the audience. Their excitement reverberated back to the stage. It was palpable. I felt myself amplified as if possessed by their collective passions. They played us, as we played them. At its height there was no performer, and no audience. There was only the music.

Upon graduation, I chose to go into music full-time. Our group had signed a recording contract with a major label and seemed poised for success. My father, obviously displeased to see the prodigal son heading off into the unsavory world of rock and roll rather than law school did his best to dissuade me, but after testing my commitment, supported me by purchasing new equipment for the band. Nevertheless, a few years in the professional music world proved to be enough.

The scene was packed with glamour, sex, and drugs, but I found myself sitting in hotel rooms after the gigs reading Zen Buddhism and Krishnamurti. The more "successful" we became, the less I experienced the heartful, tribal communion that was what I really loved about rock and roll. I left the band, deciding that I was done with being a "professional musician."

My subsequent work in the world has been a journey through many forms—clinical psychologist, business executive, lecturer and seminar leader, organizational consultant and executive coach, healer and citizen diplomat, husband and father—but at another level, it has always been about music. For I am always listening to the inner music of life, playing with forms and improvisation, savoring dissonance while seeking harmony, modulating timbres and dynamics, putting forth melody and inviting counterpoint, feeling the rhythm and grooving with the beat, always listening for the silence between the notes, striving to serve the creative impulse that moves through each moment of life.

People sometimes ask me, "How did you get into chant?" Looking back on our lives, we can sometimes see patterns that were not so obvious while we lived them. Long before I consciously set foot on the spiritual path, it was as if I had been in training to do sacred music. I had developed all the necessary musical skills, but more importantly, I had learned how to use the power of music to touch heart and soul, to invite participation and build a sense of communion among people—whether leading folk songs around the campfire, conducting classical chorales, jamming at tribal rock concerts, or chanting at political rallies.

Although I believe strongly in the power of choice, sometimes I wonder, "Are we all living a story that was, in some way, already written?" For my twenty-second birthday, my friends bought me a reading with a well-known local psychic. I approached this meeting with some skepticism, fostered from years in the psychology labs of Harvard's William James Hall. I walked into the psychic's apartment, taking in the Asian-looking bedspreads draped on the walls and tables cluttered with occult objets d'art. Before I even sat down, she asked me, "Have you learned to play the piano yet in this lifetime?"

My first reaction was, "This is a setup—my friends fed her information!" But no, as it turned out, she was for real. The reading primarily spoke of my musical abilities, but in particular of how they would affect my future. "You will be bringing to the world a great gift of music, but it is a different kind of music. It is a music whose purpose is to heal and awaken rather than to entertain. You will be a leader among those who help to birth this music for a New Age, a form of music that is both ancient and modern." At the end of the session she said, "This won't make sense to you for a while, but listen again to the tape I have made for you in ten years, and you will see."

I lost the tape for some years in one of those boxes of unsorted things that followed me from one basement to the next. The reading long forgotten, the tape resurfaced some years later. Turning on the cassette player, I listened to the diaphanous voice of the psychic predict, in advance, an astonishingly accurate history of the last ten years of my life as a sacred musician and leader of chant.

In the spring following the reading, my wife Judith and I attended a ten-day yoga retreat led by Swami Satchidananda in Connecticut. Although we had taken some yoga classes and had begun reading spiritual books, this was our first real immersion into the spiritual path. Within the first few days, I was profoundly taken with the feeling that I had come home. And while I eagerly took to both the yoga and meditation, it was, not surprisingly, the chanting that made the strongest impression. The words were now Sanskrit rather than English, but I felt like I had been chanting all my life. And I had.

Within days of my return, I was leading others in singing "Om Shanti" and began to write my first "spiritual" songs. Soon after, I joined the "house band" at weekly Sufi dancing in Cambridge, playing and singing chants of all traditions—Hindu, Buddhist, Christian, Hebrew, and Islamic. I had found my new musical calling. For me, chanting combined the warmth and communality of a sing-along, the ecstasy of a rock concert, the devotion of worship, and the stillness of meditation. In the coming years I would be exposed to many different traditions of chant. Each has its own unique ambiance and flavor, and yet for me, the Spirit at the heart of each tradition has always been the same.

Some years later, my wife and I created a weekend seminar called "Opening the Heart," a blend of humanistic psychology and spiritual practices. Chanting was an important part of the experience, and participants regularly asked for a tape of the songs to take home with them. In 1980, I recorded a simple cassette called "Many Blessings" with a group of friends and staff of the workshops. We turned on a tape recorder as we sang our favorite chants in the barn of Spring Hill, our hilltop conference center in rural Massachusetts. Our aspirations were modest and the recording quality was worlds away from the forty-eight-track studios and digital editing I use today. A discerning ear can even pick out the sounds of logs falling in the woodstove as we chanted.

We had so much fun singing together that we kept on doing it. Calling ourselves "On Wings of Song," year by year our musical quality improved, our number of singers grew, and so did the size of our audiences. We brought our unique blend of tribal rock, "message" songs, and chant in ecstatic participatory events called "transformances" to conferences, spiritual gatherings, concert halls— even to the Pentagon in an unusual performance covered by NPR's "All Things Considered." Wherever we journeyed, diverse groups of people found their common heart and found a shared way to pray through chant. But, while we continued to make recordings to sell at our concerts, we were repeatedly told by distributors of the nascent New Age music genre that "vocal music just doesn't sell."

A number of years later, I received a call very late one night at our new home in the Rocky Mountains above Boulder, Colorado. A man named John Paul was calling from England, representing a well-known author and seminar leader. One of their students had taken our five-minute version of the Sanskrit chant *Om Namaha Shivaya* from our original "Many Blessings" tape and made a tape loop. It turned out that hundreds of people were chanting along with the tape in seminars around the world, reporting powerfully transcendent experiences. John Paul wanted to know if we would make a high-quality ninety-minute tape for their organization to use and sell at their workshops.

My first reaction was, "What a dumb idea! Who would ever want to listen to ninety minutes of the same song over and over again?" Fortunately, I didn't listen to myself and agreed to create the tape, assuming it would be sold only through their seminars. Much to my amazement, within months after shipping the first tapes, the world came beating at our door. Stores around the globe contacted us, wanting copies of the tape. All of the distributors who had been passing on our music for years suddenly began calling us with urgent requests to carry *Om Namaha Shivaya.* From this inauspicious beginning, our simple tape of this traditional sacred chant grew into a worldwide phenomenon.

While some people seem to birth projects out of a flash of visionary insight, I stumbled into it. Suggestions started coming for other chanting tapes, and I immersed myself in the work of making the sacred songs of other cultures accessible to Western audiences, riding a rising tide of interest in the ancient practice of chanting.

My continuing commitment to this work is partly fueled by the ongoing stream of letters we receive from all over the world from people whose lives have been touched by these recordings of chant—heartfelt stories of chants being played for people during births, surgery, times of healing, and the passage of death. One of my favorite letters came scrawled on a dirty piece of paper from India. In barely comprehensible English, a swami from an ashram in the Himalayan foothills was requesting a donation of an *Om Namaha Shivaya* cassette for his temple. A passing Westerner had given our contemporary version of their own traditional chant to the local monks, who had so fallen in love with it that they had worn out the tape.

I feel blessed that something I love so much can bring such joy and well-being to people all over the world. I have used chanting to help groups as diverse as corporate executives and laborers, people dying from AIDs and physicians, the rich and the homeless, born-again Christians and New-Agers, and Arab and Israeli schoolchildren find a communion of heart and a connection to Spirit.

Again and again I have been told, "You'll never get them to sing," or "Our people aren't into this spiritual stuff." But I've always gone ahead and simply invited people to open their voices and open their hearts, and always, whether in corporate meeting rooms or maximum-security prisons, the streets of Moscow or the inner courtyard of the Pentagon, people have joined together in chant and in Spirit. Every one of us desires peace, love, wholeness, and a connection to something larger than ourselves. This longing, whether or not we ever think of it as spiritual, lives in each one of our hearts. And chant offers us a real and immediate opportunity to taste of this peace, to feel this love, and to experience a connection to each other and to Spirit.

Why Chant?

We chant to join our voices to the voices of countless seekers, worshipers, mystics, and lovers of life, in every time and in every place, who have shared in sacred song.

We chant to fill our hearts and fill our homes with loving and peaceful vibrations of sound.

We chant because it's fun.

We chant to help the stress and freneticness of our busy lives melt away.

We chant to spread our wings and let our soul take flight.

We chant for the sheer joy of letting our God-given voices sing out.

We chant for the heartful communion that we feel with others when we come together in song.

We chant our prayers to God, so that our lives may be graced by more intimate Presence of the One known by so many names.

What Is a Chant?

This is an intriguing question, as chant encompasses such a stunningly wide array of musical expression. From the Latin word *cantare* meaning "to sing," chant can weave beautiful melodies that send the heart soaring as we hear in some of the recent recordings of Celtic chanting. Some chant melodies have been carefully preserved over centuries, perhaps painstakingly transcribed by quill pen on parchment by a tonsured monk, and are always sung in precisely the same tonal sequence. In contrast, the Orthodox Jewish *davennen* (the traditional Jewish form of chanted prayer), while adhering to specific conventions regarding melodies, is somewhat more improvisational, treating the traditional melodies like jazz "riffs," altering rhythms to fit the changing text into the melody, and subtly adding musical embellishment. Relying on traditional melody completely gives way to the creative Spirit as Pentecostals bring forth spontaneous outpourings of sacred sound in their practice of speaking in tongues. Other forms eschew melody altogether. For example, Tibetan Buddhist monastic chant often drones on only one fundamental tone; or in the case of some Sufi *zhikrs*, the repetitive text is chanted on a half-spoken tone of indistinct pitch.

Much chant is rhythmic, from the pounding heartbeat of Native American drums, to the polyrhythmic chants of West Africa, to the incredibly complex rhythmic patterns of the Balinese Monkey Chant. On the other extreme, chant may consist of long sustained notes with no rhythm at all, as in the traditional toning of the well-known Sanskrit sacred syllable "OM." We sometimes chant extensive recitations of traditional texts such as the Buddhist Heart Sutra, the Hindu Gurugita, and the Lutheran Worship Service, but chant is also the pure vibrations of wordless tones and overtones. Chant may be the a capella voices of monks singing Gregorian chant, while other chanters are accompanied by drums and rattles, flutes and whistles, harmoniums and tambouras, bells, bowls, harps, and the unique timbres of the countless other instruments indigenous to every culture.

Chants serve many purposes: telling stories such as the mythic tale of Lord Rama and Sita in the great Indian epic the *Ramayana,* casting out disease in the healing chants of the Siberian shaman, instructing young family members in the proper patterns for fine Kashmiri carpets, or inducing trance in Haitian voodoun. Chant is used to quiet the mind, open the heart, uplift the Spirit, and mourn the dead.

Having tasted the incredible richness of the world of chant, we see that dictionary definitions are either incorrect—"a simple liturgical song in which a string of syllables or words is sung to each tone," or absurd — "any monotonous song." For our purposes, let us define chant as: the worship and celebration of the sacred through melodically simple vocalization.

Chant is singing our prayers. Chant is vocal meditation. Chant is the breath made audible in tone. Chant is "discovering Spirit in sound."

Chanting and the Body

I believe that one of the reasons chanting has such a powerful effect on practitioners is because it affects us physically as well as spiritually. Our breathing is fundamental to the way we feel in our body, and the repetitive nature of chanting induces us to breathe deeper, slower, and more rhythmically. The sound vibrations caused by making vocal sounds resonate throughout our bodies — as though we were being massaged from the inside out. Our brain-wave patterns are measurably altered, evoking states of relaxation, or heightened creative energy. Our muscle tension relaxes and skin temperature changes; our blood pressure and heart rate go down. A regular practice of chanting can elicit the relaxation response, reduce stress, sharpen mental clarity, open and expand all of our senses, and help support our overall health and wellness.

From the perspective of Eastern thought, chanting is a powerful vehicle for freeing up the vital energy of the body-mind — called *chi*, *prana*, or *kundalini* — by helping to infuse every system, organ, and cell of our body with life force. While contemporary Western medicine is only slowly opening to the possibility of vital energies playing a role in the physical body and its health, these forces (and the power of chanting) have long been recognized in other societies and systems of healing.

Because chanting has a direct impact on our body and our energy, as with acupuncture, chiropractic, and massage, we receive many of its benefits whether or not we "believe in chanting." I once hired a young sound engineer who had no previous experience with chant, toning, or anything "spiritual" to help us do a live recording of On Wings of Song. He monitored the concert from his mobile studio parked outside the hall, listening through his headphones. When I asked him afterward how the recording came out, he answered, "I'm sorry, but there may be some problems with the very end of the concert. You made these really weird noises [I had chanted a series of three high tones designed to awaken spiritual energies], and it was like bolts of electricity were shooting up my spine. I went to this incredibly beautiful place and felt things that are hard to describe— but I'm afraid I totally forgot about the recording for a while." Research has also shown that similar "nonbelievers" experience measurable physical changes ranging from a reduction in the production of stress-related hormones to increased levels of critical proteins such as interleukin-1 through the practice of chanting.

Chanting in Groups

In churches, temples, mosques, ashrams, and kivas, people are joining voices in communal worship. In forests and fields, by the sea and on mountaintops, as the sun rises and falls into dusk, human beings add their voices to the symphony of natural sounds. In the grace before meals and the quiet moments before bed, at marriages and leave-takings, at the great transitions of births and deaths, people join together to intone their prayers. At workshops and conferences, public meetings and informal gatherings, in hotel ballrooms and intimate living rooms, people in cultures where traditional forms have lost meaning are rediscovering the power of chant.

Religions and armies, tribes and nations, political marches and sports teams have all recognized and made use of the power of chant to touch our collective minds and hearts—for better and for worse. Something happens when we chant together, when we choose to give our voices, our energy, and our hearts to a common song and to each other. The experience that follows is a product of both the intention with which we come together, and the chant that is the chosen vehicle. The group that chants "De-fense, De-fense," or "Charge!" at a sporting event will go to a different place than the people holding hands and singing, "From thee I receive, to thee I give." Even within the context of sacred chant, the energy created by spirited Sanskrit *kirtan* building to its ecstatic climax is literally a world apart from that of the slowly echoing melodic lines of Gregorian chant sung by Benedictine monks at *vespers*.

In group chant, our worship comes out of the closet. We sit, we stand, or we dance, shoulder to shoulder or arm in arm with our brothers and sisters, giving voice to our deepest yearnings—together. We bear witness to each other, but more than that, we share our life force. Our attention may wander or our energy start to wane, but we are inspired by the commitment and lifted by the passion of those around us.

In chanting with groups, we have the opportunity to relax the control and open the boundary behind which we isolate ourselves from others and from life. It has been my joy and privilege to guide many, many groups in discovering the magic of chanting. I have watched people come to the chant unsettled, the aftereffects and incompletions of the day's experiences clinging to their energy field like dust and briars to a traveling cloak. I have watched people begin to sing, hesitant and shy, as if afraid lest their voice be noticed by some imaginary tribunal and judged inadequate.

The transformation that occurs when we give ourselves to chant is as predictable as the rise of the sun or the coming in of the tide. Yet it is no less a miracle. Disparate voices begin to touch each other, their multitude of tones searching for a common vibration. We breathe together, and the silence in between the musical phrases grows quieter and crystalline. Securely held in the repeating form of the chant, we become free to let the Spirit of the chant take us where it may.

And as we give ourselves to the chant, we let go into an ever-changing river of melody and movement, patterns weaving and disappearing, feeling and emptiness, sound and silence. And if we are so graced, there are moments seemingly out of time when something happens—when the boundaries that separate "me" from "you" disappear. There may seem to be but one breath that breathes through us all, voices so attuned that it seems but one voice is singing, and a joining of hearts in deep communion.

Chanting as spiritual Practice

In addition to its very direct effects on our energy and physical bodies, chanting is, as we have just seen, a powerful, historically proven tool for transforming consciousness.

Most of us suffer from a chronic case of "monkey mind." Our mind seems to have a life of its own, frantically jumping from one thing to the next. Our body is driving in our car, but our minds are all over the place. . . . I don't think that last meeting went very well. . . . I'd really like to take a vacation this winter. . . . Traffic's slow today. . . . Maybe Mexico. I saw an ad last week for discount tickets. . . . I'm hungry. What's for dinner? . . . I wonder if we'll get the contract? That new assistant is really cute. . . . I hope I'm not late because of the traffic. . . . Her blouse was a little revealing. . . . I really should meditate more often. . . .

Those of you who have practiced meditation know all-too-well the relentless energy of monkey mind. While learning to deal with mental chatter is a normal part of meditation practice, chanting is an extremely effective way of calming the mind and focusing our energy.

From a musicological standpoint—let's face it—chanting can be kind of monotonous. My father's first reaction to *Om Namaha Shivaya* was, "Hey, you should market it as an aid for insomniacs. It puts me to sleep right away—it's the most boring music I ever heard!" While chant may or may not be appreciated by those listening for musical sophistication or high performance quality, countless people are chanting and listening to chant for its effect on who we are and how we feel.

When I sit down to chant, I may be restless or tired, happy or upset, inspired or listless. Then I begin to sing. Sometimes there's an almost instantaneous sense of clicking in. I give myself to the chant, and I am touched and engaged—body, heart, and soul. Other times, that "click" is more elusive. I'm chanting, but my mind is drifting. But in the actual *practice* of chanting, we stay with it, whether our concentration is strong or scattered, our experience pleasant or uncomfortable. We keep coming back to the chant, singing, giving ourselves to the words and the tones.

The repetitive sounds of chant vibrate in our brains, again and again, washing our minds, our own wavelengths gradually coming into resonance with the tone and feeling of the musical prayer. Our bodies and energy start to beat with the rhythm of the chant, the repeating pulses start to shift our sense of being into a more aligned, more harmonious state. As we continue, we move in and out of experiences of more or less immersion in the chant. Sometimes it's clearly "me" sitting here, chanting *Om Namaha Shivaya* or *Alleluia*. Other times, we touch moments where the separation between chanter and the chant, the sense of "me" doing something fades away. There is only "chanting," and I am a part of it.

Not only is chanting a form of meditation itself, but it is an extremely useful adjunct to other meditation practices. Because of its powerful ability to shift states of consciousness, chanting may serve as a helpful bridge between our more active lives of answering the phone and getting the kids off to school, and deeper states of meditation.

In many traditions, chant is also a devotional practice—a form of heartfelt prayer. We call out to God, we honor God, we thank, we beseech, we invoke, we bow, we bless, and we celebrate. We become as intoxicated troubadours, singing our love songs to the divine Beloved:

> "Listen, listen, listen to my heart's song.
> I will never forget you, I will never forsake you."
> —*Paramahansa Yogananda*

The power of devotional chanting comes from throwing ourselves in wholeheartedly. We harness our longing for truth, our desire to know God, and our love for life and chant as if we were singing for our lives. Which we are. And in the fire of our chanting, or in the sweet silence as the last tones fade into nothingness, we may begin to actually feel such spiritual abstractions as love or oneness.

> "As the Godhead strikes the note,
> Humanity sings.
> The Holy Spirit is the harpist,
> And all the strings must sound
> which are touched in love."
> —*Mechtild of Magdeburg*
> *Thirteenth century*
> *Catholic lay sister*

We do not call Spirit into being through our chanting—God is already present. It is our own clinging to who we think we are that gets in the way. But if we sing with great ardor, our controlling, grasping, anxious energies may be consumed in the fire of chanting. And if we are so graced, we may taste love's sweet nectar and be nestled in the invisible embrace of the Divine.

About This Book

It is my hope that this book will serve you as a useful and friendly guide to the ancient and sacred practice of chanting.

We will continue our journey in chapter 2 by exploring the nature of sound and how it impacts our lives, for good and for ill. Drawing on contemporary science and traditional spiritual wisdom, we will seek to understand how invisible and intangible sound can have such strong effects on physical matter and our consciousness.

In chapter 3, we will focus on how music and specifically chant harness the power of sound for physical healing and to bring joy and the presence of Spirit into our lives. We will learn about the miraculous instrument of our own voice, toning and harmonics, mantras and sacred syllables, and music as healer.

Chapter 4, called "Common Threads," is a journey into the use of chant and ritual in cultures around the globe, drawing on the personal stories of chant leaders, swamis, lamas, shamans, singing ministers, rabbis, and priests.

For those of you interested in bringing the power of chant into your daily lives, chapter 5 will help you learn to chant with simple exercises designed to teach you the basics. By practicing while driving in your car, taking a shower, or in personal daily rituals, your life, too, can be filled with the power of sacred sound.

In chapter 6, "The Communion of Sound," we listen to stories about the power of chant in groups—from family and friends gathered around a deathbed, to couples seeking to enhance their sexual union, to On Wings of Song bringing its message of peace to the Pentagon.

Chapter 7 explores how you can use ritual and chant to imbue the events, the cycles, and passages of your life with meaning and Spirit.

In our last chapter, "Discovering Spirit in Sound," we explore the spiritual dimension of chanting. Drawing on the wisdom and stories of leaders from different traditions, we learn how to use chant as meditation and as a spiritual practice to bring our lives more in tune with the music of Spirit.

In writing a book on "Discovering Spirit in Sound," I have faced the dual challenges of having to write about Spirit, the true experience of which is beyond words, and writing about chant, whose real power is revealed only in the making and hearing of it. This book, therefore, relies on stories, for stories make the abstract and intangible come to life. It is filled with the experiences of people like yourself who have brought Spirit through sound into daily life through chanting.

Chanting Is for Everyone

Whether you are an experienced singer or the person who was asked not to sing in the class play, you can share in the wonder of chant. Chanting is not "singing"—it's about breath, about heart, and about Spirit, and we all come fully equipped to participate. It is my hope that through reading this book, you will be inspired to invite the Spirit of chant to fill your heart and home with joy.

Chapter Two

The Power of Sound

"Before the world was, all was in sound.
God was in sound, we are made of sound."
—Hazrat Inayat Khan
The Mysticism of Sound and Music

The Mystic and the Mountain Climber

Allaudin Mathieu, master musician and Sufi teacher, once told me this story about the power of chant to move mountains:

He and thirty others who were attending a summer Sufi camp in the French Alps took to the mountains one bright morning, singing mantras as they hiked. Wearing spiritual white clothes, mountain boots, and colorful scarves, the group climbed with voices ringing "Allah, Allah!" and "O Life! O Truth!" in Arabic. The trail led them to a cirque—a huge, resonant bowl-shaped space scooped out of the rock by ancient glaciers. Allaudin's idea was to sing breath's worth of "Allah" at top volume and listen for the echo. "Al-laaaaaaah!" "The sound was orgasmic," he said, "but the echo was even better. Our chord came back to us like the wake of a boat we had hurled across the glistening ocean of snow and stone. Many choirs ricocheted from the granite galleries. We sang another chord and again the cirque sang back. We thought it was the craziest, juiciest human sound ever to resound from a mountain."

The echo got even better as they continued. "Allaaaaaaah!" The Sufis were ecstatic. "We even imagined we could hear our vibrations coming back to us as a kind of human scream for God." The echo returned again, . . . but wait! This time the scream was in French! Staring across the gorge, they saw six black dots against the white snow almost a mile away. Mountain climbers. They sang another "Allah," and the returning sound was louder, again in French, but now they could understand the words. "Arrêtez! Pour l'amour de Dieu! Arrêtez! Arrêtez!" ("Stop! For the love of God! Stop! Stop!") "The climbers were yelling at us to stop our mountain music. They were begging for their lives." Unlike the Sufis, the Frenchmen understood that these loud sounds of devotion could start an avalanche. It was then that Allaudin became aware of the two-fold power of sound, and that "one man's cosmic chord could be another man's white death." He and the others immediately stopped singing. Thoughtful and subdued, they turned back down the mountain.*

The terrified French mountain climbers were justified in their fears. Did you know that ski areas actually take preventive action against avalanches by triggering loose snow through the use of sound? (They tend to use guns rather than chant.)

As you can see, sound has the power to move mountains and other matter, as well as souls. For most of my life, I have used and witnessed the power of sound, music, and chant. And yet, sometimes it still seems mysterious — even miraculous. What is actually happen-

---

* A full version of Allaudin's story can be found in his book *The Musical Life*. See the resource section for a full reference.

ing here? How can something as invisible and intangible as sound affect us so strongly?

To answer this question, we must begin by trying to understand the nature of sound itself. Even though sound is invisible, you routinely experience its undeniable power to affect your physical world and well-being. Have you ever felt furniture vibrate in your living room from the bass sounds coming from your stereo? Or sat in a dentist's chair while the technician removed plaque from your teeth using only sound waves? Have you ever recoiled from the visceral sound waves of a low-flying jet? It is this same kind of force that imbues chant with its power to touch our minds, hearts, and bodies.

Sound Is Everywhere

We are enveloped in sound. The vibrations of energy that we call sound pour through us whether we are asleep or awake, in the middle of a clangorous traffic jam, or sitting quietly by a country stream. Our bodies resonate with the thrumming of refrigerators and computers, the laughter of children, and the soft rustle of curtains as a summer storm brews outside our window.

Some sounds are perceived as beautiful, harmonious music that can cause the hairs on our arms to stand on end, bring tears to our eyes, and propel us to ecstasy. Other sounds may be experienced as disturbing, even tissue-damaging, noise. We're jangled by shrill horns, startled by unexpected cries in the night, and assaulted by the rumble of motorcycles in need of new mufflers. And if we somehow managed to block out all these external sounds, we would then become aware of another world of sound: the pulsing of blood in our veins, our beating heart, the in-and-out of life-giving breath. . . . Sound is everywhere; it surrounds and fills us every second, every hour, every day of our lives.

I have sometimes toyed with the question, "If I were forced to live without one sense, which would I choose—the sense of sight, or the sense of hearing?" Our lives are, in many ways, sight dominant, and for most of us the fear of blindness runs deep. But try to imagine a world without sound, a world without the warm and familiar voices of those you love, a world without the song of a bird or the purr of a cat, a world without the sounds of waves breaking against the shore, the wind rustling in the leaves, or water trickling in a brook. Imagine a world without music. Nineteenth-century philosopher Lorenz Oken once wrote, "The eye takes a person into the world. The ear brings the world into a human being."

The Importance of Sound

We see the profound importance of sound directly reflected in human development. Hearing is the first sense that develops in utero, with fetuses reacting to their mother's voice and other external sounds as early as four and a half months prior to birth. After birth, infants will respond to music that they heard prenatally, while failing to acknowledge other songs that they haven't yet heard. Newborns also show a distinct preference for the voice of their birth mothers— the one they have heard most consistently in the womb.

Newborns come equipped with an intact and fully functioning auditory system—in fact, the only bones fully formed at birth are those of the middle ear. Clear vision, by contrast, takes months to develop. Very soon after your birth, you could localize sounds—a highly complex task requiring differentiation of timing and volume.

We are also, from the very beginning, makers of sound. Our first daughter, Leila, like each of our three children, was born at home, birthed in a room filled with candles, chanting, and love. With her first breath, she greeted life with a series of healthy loud wails, and beginning with this first vocalization, Leila, like all infants, delighted in her own vibrating, reverberating sounds. At about eight weeks of age, she began to babble in earnest, and in those sweet, laughter-filled gurgles lay the complex seeds of language and of music. Over time, as Leila began to take in and mirror the many human sounds in our extended family, more and more, her adorable "baby talk" contained recognizable words. Beginning around twelve months, she began to elongate vowels and shift pitch in ways that were distinctly musical. Finally, after many, many more months of eagerly teaching Leila to talk, Judith returned one day from a long car ride exhausted. "Now I can't get her to stop. She talked up a blue streak for two hours. Where's the off switch?"

Infants also express an immediate interest in music. Like parents in all cultures, Judith and I would often sing to our children. I could sense their small bodies literally drinking in the sounds and vibrations of our voices, as if they were being bathed in love. I recently went to visit our friends Ron and Toby just a few days after the birth of their daughter. As I lightly fingerpicked chords on the guitar and began to softly chant, the young being immediately turned her face toward the music. For as long as I chanted, she swam in the air as if trying to crawl and nestle into the music.

Sound is food for our body and soul. Well-known French physician and researcher Alfred Tomatis (sometimes called the "Einstein of the Ear") calls sound a critical nutrient for our brain growth, as it stimulates and charges the neocortex with electrical impulses. Sound brings us to attention and keeps us awake. It is the basis of language development and guides us in communication. But far more than just a mechanism for hearing, our auditory system also orchestrates the brain and nervous system to enable us to talk, stay erect, and move. The auditory system is connected to every muscle in the body, inter-acts with the cranial nerves that send information to and from the brain, and maintains balance and orientation in space. Tomatis's research indicates that insufficient or unhealthy exposure to sound in our formative years retards our development in all of these areas. Without sufficient charging through sound, in a sense the brain becomes "malnourished."

If sound is such a critical nutrient, you may well wonder how it is that the hearing-impaired are not starving. It turns out that in addition to being received through our ears, sound vibrations also enter the body directly through the skin, hair, and the bones themselves. My son and I went to hear Japanese Taiko drummers on the Boulder Mall one summer evening. As they ceremonially pounded their thick wooden sticks on the massive drums, our bodies were instantly struck by a wall of vibration. We experimented with blocking our ears. Even without any sound entering our ears, we still had a full-body experience of the music, our ribs and sternum pulsing in time with the beats, every inch of our skin tingling rhythmically.

You can easily demonstrate this for yourself by playing some music on your stereo and turning up the volume. Now, place your fingertips on the very front of the speakers and notice how you "feel the music." Incredible as it may seem, there are a number of world-class musicians who, though completely unable to hear, have performed in orchestras solely through the ability to feel vibration.

Sound is a nutrient for our Spirit as well as our body. It is how we express ourselves to the world. And sound in the form of music accompanies us throughout our lives, celebrating our brightest moments, sensualizing our romances, and offering comfort for our pain. As we shall see, many spiritual traditions hold sound to be the direct expression of the Divine power that creates form from endless space. Sufi master Hazrat Inayat Khan writes, "This sound is the source of all manifestation. . . . The knower of the mystery of sound knows the mystery of the whole universe."

What Is Sound and How Do We Hear It?

Sound is scientifically defined as any vibratory disturbance in the pressure and density of a medium (solid, liquid, or gas) that stimulates the sense of hearing. When molecules in gases are moved—by someone speaking, a pebble dropping into a pond, a hammer pounding a nail, or voices joined in chant—energy is transferred, and the molecules begin to tremble and collide. As they bump together, each shimmering molecule passes energy along to its neighbors, carrying this vibration through the air (or other medium) in the form of a three-dimensional wave.

We take our ability to hear sounds for granted, but it is actually a wild and complex process. Something happens out there to start air molecules vibrating, forming a wave of sound. Let's imagine for a moment that you are this sound wave. Air molecules crash into each other like billiard balls, causing you to surge and roll through space, like an ocean wave traveling toward shore. You enter a funnel-shaped appendage we call the outer ear, where you are amplified and tossed onto the tympanic membrane—the eardrum—causing it to vibrate. No longer a sound wave, you have been transformed into mechanical energy, setting in motion the three tiniest bones in the body—the bones of the middle ear: the hammer, the anvil, and the stirrup. You collide into the hammer, forcing it into a cuplike socket on the anvil, causing the stirrup to act like a piston pressing against the fluid-filled, spiraling labyrinth that is the inner ear. As you swirl through liquid, you reach the inner ear and snake your way through a snail-shaped tube—the cochlea—which contains fine hairlike projections that trigger nerve cells. Now you are electrical energy speeding to the brain through the auditory nerve. Countless neutrons are triggered, associations made, and . . . amazingly . . . someone hears.

Before we can truly learn to chant, we must learn to listen more deeply and open ourselves to the invisible world of audible vibrations we call sound. As we shall see, the power of chant lies as much in receiving the vibrations of the tones produced by ourselves and others as it does from our own singing. Here is our first exercise, designed to help sensitize your ability to listen.

∞ ∞ ∞

Exercise #2–1 Listening

This exercise works best if you try it in three steps. Read the directions for the first step, and then close your eyes.

• Step One

Bring all of your attention to the experience of listening.

What is the first sound that you become aware of?

There is a label by which we identify this sound—traffic, refrigerator, people talking, birds. . . . But what's really happening? What is your actual experience of this sound? The actual physical sensations?

Immerse yourself fully in this experience called "a sound." Then, as if you are increasing magnification with a zoom lens, listen more closely to that sound. As if you could travel inside the sound, let it become your whole world. Take your time. Explore every sensation.

• Step Two

This time, rather than focusing on one sound, listen to all the sounds in your environment.

Some are louder—more in the foreground. Some are softer—in the background and harder to discern. Sounds come at you from all different directions—in front, behind, maybe even above or below. How many different sounds can you hear?

And now, rather than hearing individual sounds, hear all of these sounds at once. Imagine you are listening to an orchestra, and each of these sounds is one of the instruments. Listen to all the sounds in your environment as if they fit together beautifully into a piece of music. Sit back and enjoy the performance.

• Step Three

Choose one sound to focus on again.

Where are you hearing this sound? Does it seem like the sound is out there? But where does the experience of listening actually take place? Out there? In your ear? In your brain?

Imagine some event out there causing air molecules to vibrate. Imagine sound waves traveling toward your body . . . entering your ear . . . becoming mechanical vibrations in bones . . . becoming neuroelectrical impulses . . . triggering associations in your brain. Imagine all this going on, creating the miracle we call sound.

∞ ∞ ∞

When I take the opportunity to really listen, I am always amazed at the range and richness of the world of sound. Like a continually shifting tapestry, the sound landscape warps and wefts, weaving in and out, winding tighter together . . . now opening to create space . . . continually changing a kaleidoscope of patterns.

You will notice that some sounds seem higher—the song of a bird, the rustle of papers, or the sound of a flute. Other sounds appear lower—the rumble of thunder, a truck motor idling outside your open window, or the thump-thump of an electric bass. What we experience as the pitch of a sound is determined by its frequency—the number of sound-wave crests that pass by a given point in one second. The higher the frequency of a sound wave—the more rapidly the waves are moving—the higher the pitch. Frequency is expressed in cycles per second called Hertz (abbreviated Hz).

From a universal range of sound that includes *billions* of frequencies, those of us with normal hearing can perceive and interpret only within a tiny spectrum—from 20 to 20,000 Hz—about ten octaves. This range tends to diminish with age, nerve loss, or injury, particularly among the higher frequencies, which is why it is often difficult to make out individual conversations amidst "cocktail party" noise as we get older.

There is a vast universe of sound beyond the range of our limited capacities to hear. Animals such as dolphins and bats inhabit unimaginably rich sonic environments, filled with their own high-frequency sound emissions used to navigate. The air around us ripples with the unheard sounds of electricity, microwaves, radar, television signals, and radio broadcasts, some ranging as high as one billion Hz.

Another interesting characteristic of sound waves is that they are, theoretically, eternal. The decay rate of sound waves is one of those paradoxical equations that approaches zero, but never arrives. Imagine that a bell is struck—ringing, resounding, and now fading. If we are very quiet, we can still hear the last tones hanging in the silence. Now it has stopped. Or has it? If we use a microphone, the bell will be audible after our unassisted ear can no longer hear it. And after that tone fades, we can turn up the input gain and once again, the sound seems to reappear. And after it fades beyond the range of our amplification system, beyond the threshold of our hearing, still the tone continues. Sound waves grow weaker and weaker, but on some level, never entirely disappear.

Consider the thousands of words you speak each day. All the words you have uttered in this lifetime—their echoes are reverberating still. Makes us want to pause before we speak! When we chant, we are consciously sending out positive tones of peace and healing into a world all too often resounding with the echoes of fear, pain, and violence.

The Positive Impact of Sound

The pioneering work of Alfred Tomatis has shown the powerful effects of treating the nervous system with sound. His extensive research demonstrates that certain types of high-frequency sounds energize or "charge" the nervous system and stimulate the muscles of the middle ear, while other low-frequency ones deplete or "discharge" it. In sound clinics, practitioners of his healing modality have successfully treated a wide variety of human problems including depression, learning disabilities, sleep disorders, and extreme neurological injuries by "reeducating" and "feeding" the ear through charged sounds. Of particular relevance to our topic, the treatment protocols of tens of thousands of patients have included the processed sounds of chant.

The physical effects of sound healing have been demonstrated not only on humans, but with cats, dogs, and even plants. Audio cassettes have been produced that induce plants to ingest nutrients into their roots at a rate many times faster than normal, causing large — even gargantuan — growth. For some, it may be hard to believe that plants "hear" or have such a powerful reaction to sound, but researcher Dan Carlson's plant-growing efforts were recorded in the *Guinness Book of World Records* — using a special sound device, he produced a houseplant that grew to over 1300 feet in length!

Ultrasonic frequencies are harnessed for everything from sonar guidance technology that detects shapes in the ocean to the homogenization of milk. One American company has even begun using "acoustical levitation" in which high-frequency sounds are actually used to lift objects. Sounds in ultrasonic frequencies help us "see" through matter in procedures such as MRIs and echocardiography. In our family scrapbook, we proudly display our first baby picture — an ultrasound representation of Leila in utero. Modern medicine uses ultrasonic "scalpels" for delicate ear and brain surgeries. Like a modern-day Joshua blowing his trumpet to break apart the walls at the battle of Jericho, doctors also harness the power of sound to blast apart painful kidney stones and gallstones.

The Negative Impact of Sound

Sound also has the power to disrupt or harm. Among the negative environmental impacts of an expanding population and increased reliance on machines is noise pollution. Each generation seems to be exposed to increasingly higher amounts of noise. As my friend, author and musician Don Campbell, points out in his book, *The Mozart Effect,* "We are bombarded with hundreds of times more sonic vibratory information than our parents or grandparents could ever have imagined."

Sound can be measured on the basis of its loudness or intensity, described by "decibel" level and abbreviated as dB. The higher the decibel number, the louder the sound. Human beings can hear sounds as low as 0 to 5 dB—below the loudness of an average whisper (15 dB). Many of us inhabit a very noisy world where traffic zooms by at 50 dB, our offices create cacophonies of 60 dB, and sirens scream at about 120 dB. People typically begin to complain of noise at about 60 dB, while the threshold of pain is somewhere around 130 dB. Typical rock concerts emit sound vibrations that are at least 120 dB, and it's become popular among concertgoers to place an egg near the edge of the stage during particularly loud performances. By the end of the show, the egg is hardboiled and so is our hearing. More than sixty million Americans suffer from hearing loss, and noise exposure is the leading cause.

Research has shown that noise caused by traffic, aircraft, power tools, and industry interferes with communication, disturbs work and sleep, induces mental and physical stress, lowers libido, reduces learning, and diminishes the quality of life for many people. Perhaps you have had an experience of being in the presence of a constant source of noise—a loud refrigerator or air conditioner, or a truck parked outside your window. At first, we feel irritated, thinking about the noise and wishing it would stop. Then we seem to forget about it for a while. Finally, the noise stops. Only then do we become aware of how our muscles had tensed and our breathing had constricted in reaction to the noise. "Ahhh!" we sigh in relief, as we begin to relax.

Imagine this kind of sonic stress continuing for days or even years. Noise literally can make us sick. One typical study showed that preschoolers exposed to chronic sounds of traffic had physically higher blood pressure than children attending school in areas without traffic noise. Cardiovascular disease, hypertension, and high levels of stress—even some cancers—have been found to increase with increasing noise pollution. People have even attempted to intentionally harness this negative power of sound to harm. In their own somewhat ludicrous version of Jericho, the U.S. military in 1989 unsuccessfully blasted loud rock music at the headquarters of Manuel Noriega in an effort to drive him out of his sanctuary (and his presidency) in Panama.

How Sound Can Move Mountains

Sound waves send their invisible pulses of energy through air, water, and earth, literally pushing and shaping matter like waves upon the shore. A number of years ago, I saw for the first time the picture below, which, for me, graphically captures the impact of sound on matter.

At first glance, I thought it was a picture of a mandala—a circular form that is used as a point of focus in many Eastern meditation practices. To my amazement, I discovered that it was a picture of sound waves shaping matter. Building on the early work of German physicist Ernst Chladni, known as "the father of acoustics," Swiss scientist Hans Jenny created a variety of devices that allow us to "see" sound waves by illustrating their physical impact on malleable substances such as sand, iron filings, and liquids.

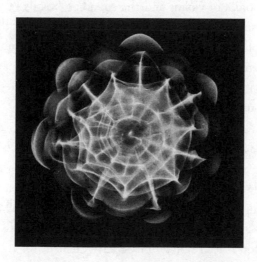

Chladni form

Sand, of course, is light and easy to move. And most sounds are not so loud as gunshots or thirty Sufis howling "Allah." The true impact of sound on our world can only be appreciated by understanding the phenomenon of *resonance*. Re-sonance means, literally, to re-sound.

Most objects, from subatomic particles to planets, have one or more frequencies at which they will naturally vibrate. When a sound wave strikes an object, if there is a match between the frequency of the wave and the frequencies inherent in the object, the object begins to vibrate. The effect of this matching of frequencies is called resonance. Small objects will be set in vibration by higher-frequency sounds; large objects resonate to low-frequency waves, such as the furniture in your house that vibrates in the presence of bass sounds coming from your stereo.

When the resonating object begins to vibrate in sync with the original wave, the wave is amplified. Sound becomes louder, its effects magnified. Without resonance, in fact, there would be no music at all. The bodies of violins and the sounding boards of pianos resonate when struck by the sound waves coming from the vibrating strings, amplifying barely audible sound vibrations into beautiful tones. A dramatic musical example of resonance is a soprano shattering a glass with her voice alone, as her frequency matches and amplifies the resonant frequency of the crystal.

Jonathan Goldman, Director of the Sound Healers Association, explains, "Sound is vibration, . . . and through resonance, it is possible for the vibrations of one vibrating body to reach out and set another body into motion." If you were to go into a music store and strike a tuning fork tuned to the note of A (440 Hz), all of the other tuning forks tuned to that note would begin to vibrate and sound. The other forks need not be physically touched, for they are being struck by the sound waves emanating from the original tuning fork.

Tuning forks tuned to notes other than A would remain still; only objects with resonant frequencies will vibrate.

The way we commonly use the word "resonance" is actually a good reflection of this important sonic concept. We say "I really resonate with her," or "That idea just doesn't resonate with me" to convey a matching or mismatching of energies, feelings, or ideas.

Sometimes bodies with different frequencies can resonate with each other as well. In 1665, Dutch scientist Christian Huygens noticed that when he mounted pendulum clocks side by side on a wall, the pendulums began to swing together in precisely the same rhythm. In other words, the clocks began to beat "in sync" with each other. In repeating Huygens's experiment, contemporary psychologist George Leonard commented that "it was as if they 'wanted' to keep the same time." Similarly, two individual muscle cells from the heart can be seen through a microscope—each pulsing to its own rhythm. But when they are moved closer together—though never touching—there is a shift, and they begin to perfectly synchronize their rhythm and beat together. This phenomenon—two entities vibrating at different frequencies coming into resonance with one another—is called *entrainment*. As we shall see in the next chapter, entrainment has profound implications for chant, but for now, let us say that there is deeper meaning to the contemporary expression, "We're on the same wavelength."

The Creative Power of Sound

The understanding that sound can shape matter is far from new. The creation myths of almost every culture show sound as the mechanism by which Spirit gives birth to the physical world. In Egyptian lore, the original god—Khepri—created first himself and then brought the world into form by calling out his own name. Plato taught that the world-soul (the cosmos) was created according to musical intervals and proportions, while the Greek god Orpheus brought forth form through his honey-sweet, magical singing. African, Australian, Polynesian, Tahitian, Hawaiian, and Japanese creation stories all reflect the belief that matter is formed and life begins through God's sounds and tones.

In the cosmology of the Native American Hopi, only Tawa (the sun god) and Spider Woman (the earth goddess) originally existed in endless space. Hearing no joyful sound and seeing no joyful movement, they decided to create living forms, and this thought became the first song. Spider Woman took clay of the four colors of the earth—yellow, red, white, and black—and mixed them with *túchvala,* the liquid of her mouth. Tawa and Spider Woman then placed a sacred blanket over these new creatures, and together they chanted them into life.

As a child, I remember reading in the book of Genesis how the world was created from a dark formless void through the sound of God's voice chanting "Let there be light." The New Testament tells us that: "In the beginning was the Word, and the Word was with God, and the Word was God. . . ." Since the original Greek word *logos* (here translated as "word") also means "sound," it would be also accurate for this famous passage to read: "In the beginning was the Sound, and the Sound was with God, and the Sound was God. . . ."

The Persian Sufi poet Hafiz tells us how God originally made a statue out of clay in His own image. He asked the soul to enter into the body. But the soul didn't like the idea of being so limited, so captive in this form. The soul preferred to fly about freely. God then asked the angels to play music, and as they did, the soul was so moved to ecstasy that it willingly entered the body in order to fully experience the music. Hafiz says, "Many say that life entered the human body by the help of music, but the truth is that life itself is music."

We often think that myths are interesting fairy tales, perhaps acknowledging them as "quaint" or "primitive" attempts to understand "reality." But in this case, there is considerable common ground between the creation myths of traditional religions and the theories of the contemporary "religion" of science. Chaitanya Kabir, a Sanskrit scholar, musician, and teacher, compares Hindu cosmology to the modern scientific paradigm. "The whole universe comes out of a single vibration," he says. "Whether we call it the 'Big Bang Theory' or we call it 'OM,' it's the same thing. There is a single vibration that went forth from pure consciousness and elaborated itself so much that, eventually, it created the impression that there are solid things here, physical things here. But even physics will tell us that almost all of the physical space of an atom or solid material is emptiness. There's just a tiny bit of matter there, and that is just waves meeting. It's waves giving the pretense of matter." In the words of the Greek philosopher Pythagoras, "A stone is frozen music, frozen sound."

Ancient ideas that sound and vibration represent the fundamental nature of reality are reflected in the theories of modern particle physics and quantum mechanics. The belief that matter is solid and unchangeable has given way to evidence showing a universe alive with complex structures of activity, patterns, energy, movement, process, relationships, and vibrations.

Quantum physicist Michio Kaku depicts the fundamental forces of particles in nature as vibrating strings of energy like the strings of a violin resonating with different frequencies or tones. "The answer to the ancient question, 'What is matter?' " he writes, "is simply that matter consists of particles that are different modes of vibration of the string, such as the note G or F. The 'music' created by the string is matter itself."

I have had experiences that reflect Kaku's theory—moments where all of life becomes a symphony of vibrating sound, pulsing and shimmering in a cosmic orchestra. I have felt the presence of that creative force called God or Spirit that in some unknowable way provides order and direction to these swirling energies. There is an underlying music that permeates all creation, with its dissonance and harmony, melodies and counterpoint, changing tempos and rhythms, elegant forms and wild improvisation. I have experienced in my body, heart, and soul the creative power of sound.

The Invisible Is Real

There is much in life that is real even though we cannot see or touch it. There exists an invisible world—of dreams and passions, of mind and thought and vision—a world of soul and Spirit. Through the instrument of our bodies, we also inhabit a visible world—a material world of physicality, a world that we can see and touch. Both of these worlds are real.

Sound is a remarkable bridge between the two worlds, a bridge between Spirit and matter. Through the vibrating energy that is sound, the invisible world can reach out and touch this physical plane. Through resonance and entrainment, sound energy can make patterns in sand, even move mountains. And as we will see in chapter 3, sound, when organized as chant, can reweave the patterning of our hearts and our souls.

Chapter Three

The Power of Chant

"Oh music,
In your depths we deposit our hearts and souls.
Thou hast taught us to see with our eyes
and hear with our hearts."
—Kahlil Gibran

It was the eve of Yom Kippur in the streets outside the Moscow synagogue, October 1983. Judith and I were traveling as members of a delegation of humanistic psychologists, attempting to build bridges with our Soviet counterparts. It was, to say the least, a tough time for a visit—a Korean jetliner carrying several hundred passengers had been shot down over Soviet airspace the previous week, and cold-war tensions were at a peak. It was also the height of Soviet repression of Jewry, and public gatherings of Jews were forbidden except in this bleak street outside the synagogue on holidays.

It was a strange scene. As many as a thousand people were milling outside, far more than the older Jews worshiping inside the temple. People were clustered in small groups, exchanging news, talking about emigration—who had gone and who was going. And everywhere, glaringly obvious KGB and police plainclothesmen were snapping photographs of people in the crowd or scribbling notes on little pads of paper, while behind wooden barricades surrounding the area, the People's Militia stood watch in their faded brown uniforms, military hats, and red armbands. Not surprisingly, the milling Jews were wearing somewhat furtive looks as they tried to take advantage of this rare opportunity to congregate.

We had come to take part in High Holy Day services, and on our way out of the synagogue we were accosted by numbers of Russian Jews, warmly curious about the Jews from *"Amereeka."* I carried my guitar, as I always do when traveling, for music to me is the greatest of emissaries.

Judith and I felt a deep tribal connection to these strangers in their strange land. Only several generations back, our grandparents had come from this part of the world. The faces of the men and women seemed very familiar—definitely from our gene pool. And they were frightened, struggling to find the courage to live, to act, and to love in conditions that we in our country of relative liberty and wealth had never had to face.

I opened my case and, on impulse, began to play . . . and sing. I performed several songs. Slowly, more and more people gathered . . . obviously wanting to come closer, yet fearful that too large a crowd might be broken up by the police. As my voice and my heart reached out to my unknown relatives, I saw a myriad of emotions reflected in their eyes—a longing for the safety and warmth evoked by the music, and wonder at the act of someone standing and singing in the face of the agents of their repression.

For me, music is a vehicle for the magic of healing and the power of Spirit. I use the word *magic,* because no matter how many times I experience the power of music and chant, there is always a sense of mystery and awe. I wished them to taste that healing and power. I wanted this group of courageous, struggling souls, even for a moment, to feel the depth of their connection to each other and their heritage, and to experience the living communion of Spirit through song—right here in the cruel streets of Moscow.

And so I began to sing some simple Hebrew chants, simple repeated melodies that some might know, and even if they didn't, could learn instantly—melodies that irresistibly evoke rich Jewish soul. Reaching out with my voice, my eyes, my heart, and the music, the listeners were invited into an experience of sound and of vibration that was warm and harmonious, an experience compelling in its vitality and soulfulness, an experience of chant.

As I chanted, I watched people, one by one, wrestle with the choice to join in. "Can I really sing out the songs of our people, right here, in a public place?" In their eyes, I saw the reflections of their struggle with years of fear and hiding. And one by one, they began to sing. Tentatively at first, their mouths almost soundlessly forming the shapes of the notes. Then a few brave voices joining mine in the center of the sound, forming a core of chant, a wave of energy, that became more and more compelling in its call. At last we were a hundred voices, chanting the ancient tunes, coming together in prayer and sound as people always have in times of peace and times of difficulty. The fear was still visibly present, yet we chanted the melody to *Hatikvah*, the song of hope, again and again, voices and hearts joining, a vibrating oasis of sound in an urban desert. Eyes (including mine) brimmed over with tears, chests swelled, and voices broke with feeling, as the magic of chant brought hope to our hearts and gave strength to our Spirits.

What happened in the streets of Moscow? How is it that chant has such profound power to move the human Spirit? We begin our search for understanding by exploring how chant impacts our physical bodies.

Chant and the Body

If you lived in the Amazon jungle and were suffering from a physical disease like cancer, or a disorder of your emotions like depression or insomnia, you might travel to see someone like shamanic healer Don Agustin Rivas-Vasquez. "It is the Spirits that do the healing, I am simply a middleman," he says with unaffected humility. Singing wordless tunes—*icaros*—then adding sacred words according to the diagnosis, he would begin a ceremony designed to help you. Some of the healing words and sounds would be chanted, others blown through the breath into a harmonica or through smoke. Musician, cross-cultural researcher, and author Pat Moffitt Cook describes the work of Don Agustin Rivas-Vasquez—and other indigenous healers—in her book *Shaman, Jhankri & Néle*. "There's a common thread among healers throughout the world that vibration underlies the way to intercept illness," she told me. Sound is recognized as a powerful healing modality because of its ability to affect vibration. "There is a sacredness in these practices, and their application is a divine act."

If you are from the urban wilds of Cleveland rather than the jungles of Brazil, you might go to see Deforia Lane, Ph.D. Shamans, as part of their initiation, traditionally struggle with their own wounding and healing, and Dr. Lane's work as founder of the music therapy program at University Hospital's Ireland Cancer Center grew directly out of her own experiences as a breast cancer survivor, in which music played an important role in her recovery. If you were to walk into the cancer clinic, you would see a very tall, attractive African American woman surrounded by her patients in varying stages of treatment, singing together, accompanying themselves with small drums and rattles, writing their own songs, radiating joy and vitality.

While initially focused on reducing depression and evoking hope and courage in her patients, like Don Agustin, Dr. Lane understands the intimate connections between mind, Spirit, and body. The medical director of the cancer center sees the power of music firsthand: "Even if we never pinpoint exactly how music heals, the effects are so positive that we know how important this program is to our patients." But Deforia Lane wants more. "In Western medicine, we value what we can measure," she says. And so this healer-scientist, like others in her field, conducts studies that investigate the power of music and chant to affect physiological changes, such as reducing the hormones responsible for the "wasting syndrome" found in cancer.

"Healing" is defined by *Webster's Dictionary* as simply "to make sound," and throughout history there has been an intimate relationship between music, health, and healing. In Greek mythology, Apollo is the god of medicine *and* of music, often depicted playing his lyre to cure sickness. His son Asclepius was considered to be the inventor of medicine and was the spiritual guardian of healing centers established throughout Greece, where music was played to restore health and refresh the Spirit. Among Eastern philosophies, the Indian goddess Sarasvati, usually seen carrying her *veena* (a South Indian stringed instrument) invented both music and medicine, while the god Shiva is frequently pictured carrying the flute with which he plays healing music.

The ancient world's understanding of music as a healing force lives on today in most indigenous cultures, where music continues to be a powerful force in the treatment of disease. The predilection of allopathic Western medicine to split mind and body into separate, unrelated domains until recently greatly inhibited the contemporary researching and practice of music as a therapeutic modality. Recent years, however, have witnessed a radical shift in our acceptance of the mind-body connection in health and healing, and music therapy has made its way from the jungles, libraries of ancient healing arts, and offices of alternative practitioners into the modern-day Asclepian temples of conventional medicine known as hospitals.

Powerful Medicine

A five-year-old girl, diagnosed with cancer, sits in a large room with her mother waiting for an appointment with the doctor. She is surrounded by other children, all of whom are fighting for their lives against this dreaded disease. On this particular day, the waiting room is lively, as the children are entertained by several adults playing guitars and leading songs.

Most of the tunes are childrens' songs, though some are whimsical and have no lyrics, only sounds. "Ahhhhh," the little girl sings, "Ohhhhmmmm." The children are bald from chemotherapy and most have thin, drawn faces, a testament to their struggle. Nevertheless, they are smiling and singing—having a good time. The music offers a welcome distraction from the endless waiting.

But more than entertainment is happening here. Researchers have taken a sample of each child's saliva before they began singing. They will take another before the children leave for the day. The study also included a control group of children who didn't participate in the music and singing. By measuring immunoglobulin levels—a highly accurate marker of immune-system functioning—the study demonstrated that the children who sang showed significant physiological changes: their immune systems were given a major boost. Children who were not placed in the singing group experienced no such change.

While some may find this scientific evidence surprising, those who have studied the effects of chanting, music, and sound on health take it as yet another confirmation of what has been known since ancient times: vocalizing has healing properties. Contemporary medical research has shown that chanting and other forms of vocalization actually oxygenate the cells, lower blood pressure and heart rate, increase lymphatic circulation, increase levels of melatonin, reduce stress-related hormones, release endorphins (the body's natural painkillers), and boost the production of interleukin-1 (a protein associated with blood and platelet production). One study conducted in Paris discovered that women with breast cancer significantly reduced or eliminated tumors through toning and chanting several hours each day for a month. From eating disorders, schizophrenia, hyperactivity, arthritis, heart disease, recovery from surgery and trauma, to Alzheimer's disease, vocal sound is proving itself to be a vibrant healing energy.*

Dr. Frederick Leboyer—well-known proponent of gentle birthing—claims that chanting during childbirth offers women the opportunity to experience childbirth holistically, creating not only healthier deliveries for mothers and infants but births endowed with great spiritual significance. My wife Judith, having been trained in childbirth classes to blow and pant to ease the pain of contractions, discovered the superiority of chanting over panting during the births of our three children. "The blowing was not enough—I needed to make sounds, particular kinds of sounds. I noticed that if I tightened my throat and made constricted sound, the birthing process also contracted. But when I allowed full and open sounds to give expression to my breath, it assisted me in opening the cervix and helping the baby down the birth canal."

On the other end of life's journey, as a psychologist in the early days of hospice, each day I removed from the black bag of my

---

* For a full helping of stories and research that demonstrate the healing power of music, I highly recommend Don Campbell's popular book *The Mozart Effect*. A full reference can be found in the resource section at the end of the book.

healers' trade my well-traveled guitar. Wandering the halls of the regional cancer center, I sang hope for those facing treatment; intoned healing balm for those in pain; helped patients and family find through chant a way to express feelings for which words came hard; created bedside oases of love where nurses, doctors, and orderlies wandered in from the hallway to share in the gift of song; and chanted rituals of grieving for those left behind when their loved ones left on their final journey.

Of many such stories, I vividly remember gathering around the bedside of my dying friend Karen: her husband, fully present and supporting her to the last; her three grieving children, torn between their desire to hold onto their mom as long as possible and her visible suffering that begged for release; her older sister, struggling with the imminent death of the one person on whom she most leaned for support and guidance; our small circle of friends, still young enough for the death of one of our own to be an assault on fleeting dreams of immortality; and myself, my many years of hospice work no shield against the sadness of saying good-bye to this dear, wise friend who had loved me so well . . . and yet determined to fulfill her soulful request of me to "please help me die."

As I began to strum my guitar, Karen's eyes began to flutter closed, taking longer and longer journeys away from the world of the living. I played softly at first, so as to not intrude on those lost in the worlds of their private thoughts and feelings. I played the chants that we all knew from traveling the paths of life together over the years:

> "May the long time sun shine upon you.
> All love surround you.
> And the pure light within you.
> Guide your way home."

Coming out of their protective cocoons of sorrow, hands reached out for one another. Voices touched one another in song, finding connection, warmth, and comfort.

> "Go in Beauty,
> Peace be with you,
> Til we meet again in the Light."

As she drifted further into her own world, we sang now to Karen, finding strength in the communion of chant to say good-bye, to release our mother/wife/sister/friend, to send her off with deep love and honoring for the wonder she was. And somewhere, imperceptibly, held in a field of such tender hearts and open Spirit, nurtured by chant, Karen slipped away.

Chant and Consciousness

While there is growing evidence of the impact of chant on physical health, it is chant's ability to affect consciousness—such as we see in the story of Karen's death—that is our primary focus. Chant can open our hearts and lift our Spirits. Chant can ease our suffering, give voice to our deepest yearnings, and give life to abstractions such as love or Spirit. Chant can help us find peace amidst a whirlwind of emotion, bring us closer to each other, and closer to God.

Whether by a dying friend's bedside, in the streets of Moscow, or sitting in our own living room, I am filled with wonder by chant's ability to penetrate our hearts and minds, how it evokes the intangible realms of Spirit. As a lifelong student and practitioner of chant, I have studied its nature and how chant works, time and time again in vastly different settings and with incredibly diverse people. I have come to believe that chant performs its magic in our consciousness by harnessing five elemental powers:

1. *Anchoring:* As memories become associated with different chants or melodies, they are released in a flood of feeling and energy whenever we sing or hear those same chants.
2. *Entrainment:* The repetitive nature of chant facilitates the entraining of our body and psyche to its rhythms and mood.
3. *Breath:* Chanting alters the way we breathe and thus the full range of mind/body functioning that is linked to breath.
4. *Sonic Effects:* The particular tonal and vibrational characteristics of chant have a direct impact on our body and energy.
5. *Intent:* While chant certainly affects us even without our conscious participation, chant has its greatest impact when we engage the power of our own desires and will.

By exploring each of these powers in turn, we will come away with a greater appreciation for how chant affects our minds and Spirits, and a better understanding of the role that it can play in our own lives.

The Power of Anchoring

The sounds of country music radiate from the small boom-box hiding behind the counter in the roadside gas station. An impatient customer scowls while hurriedly signing his credit-card slip, ill-informed stereotypes of rednecks and hillbillies dancing in his mind accompanied by the recurring thought, "I hate country music!" The person standing behind him in line hears the same sounds, but not the same music. She remembers being scrunched in the backseat of the old family car with Mom and Dad twenty years ago, listening to Loretta Lynn as the headlights of oncoming cars made patterns on the rainlashed windshield. Time-tripping through a field of warm memories, she smiles wistfully and thinks, "Ah, country music!"

The same music will affect people differently because of the associations it triggers. Music anchors our experiences of places and people. The faces and voices, the smells and tastes, the dreams and disappointments, all indelibly bind themselves to the music of that time. A song can capture a moment in our lives, preserved forever like an insect in amber. Walking barefoot in the sand, hand in hand with our sweetheart, the smell of the air, and a kiss that lingers and promises more . . . young love returns in a flood of memory years later, when a certain "oldie" comes over the radio.

Remember a song from your childhood. Hear it playing now, and remember all the memories and feelings that come with this music. Our sensory and emotional memories have been encoded to the distinctive melodies and rhythms of the music from those times and places. When we hear the music, synapses fire, making connections in our brain; hormones release into our bloodstream, stimulating emotion; the past is conjured and lives once more so long as the music plays.

This capacity of music to anchor and trigger associations explains part of its power to affect our hearts and minds. If I had played American folk songs before the Moscow synagogue, people would have been entertained but not so profoundly moved as they were by the songs of their own people and the wealth of memory and feeling connected to those melodies.

Countries, schools, political movements, sports teams—all bind people together with this associative power of music. For the French, their anthem "La Marseillaise" stirs a lifetime of feeling and identification with their homeland. Our school or camp songs may evoke a lasting bond of shared memory in alumni. "We Shall Overcome" will forever strike a common chord in those who worked for Civil Rights in the sixties, while the sentiments of their segregationist adversaries still rally to the strains of "Dixie." For a few moments in the seventh inning, "Take Me Out to the Ballgame" brings thirty thousand fans to their feet, their voices fueled by triggered memories of childhood heroes at the plate, the smell of peanuts and hot dogs, playing catch with Dad, and the day their team won the pennant.

This power also has significant potential in healing, brought home to me personally in one of my few truly life-changing events. I will always remember, at age fifteen, overhearing our family doctor tell my father that my mom had just died. My heart was already so shut down in the face of this overwhelming loss that my first thought was, "I wonder if this is a good enough excuse not to get my homework in on time?" For years afterward, my heart was frozen, unable to feel much of anything for fear of drowning in the unexpressed grief of losing my mother. After a while, I could barely remember her. Some eight years later, I was lying in bed with Judith watching a television rerun of the musical *Peter Pan*. We came to a part in the story where the orphaned Peter is trying to remember his mother. Peter turns to the other lost boys and begins singing to them the lullaby he dimly remembers being sung to him: "Once upon a time and long ago, I heard someone singing soft and low." All of a sudden, I remembered having watched this show with my mother, how my mother had sung to me, and the sound of her voice. As Peter sang, I realized that I, too, was a lost boy. And the song became the switch that opened the floodgates. In Judith's arms, I wept for the first time since I was a young child, the trickle of memories swelling to a torrent, the music melting my heart like the spring sun thaws the winter's frozen wastes. It was the beginning of my healing. Even now, when I hear this song, I feel a lump in my throat and my eyes involuntarily start to water.

The Power of Entrainment

This power of music to radically shift our consciousness and our experience is not only a result of triggering past memories. Right here in the present, the vibrations of music are impacting us through the phenomenon of entrainment. Remember the clock pendulums? Well, our bodies, heart rates, and brain waves entrain to melody and rhythm, just the way the clock pendulums entrained to one another. Think how quickly our feet start to tap in rhythm when a good dance beat starts to play. In opening ourselves to the experience of music, we to some degree *become* the music.

Music has intrinsic qualities, apart from what we may bring to it. It vibrates with a certain pulse and distinctive timbre. It may have melodies that rise or fall, harmonies that are rounder or more dissonant, attacks that are staccato or legato. As these waves of music meet the vibrations of our body and emotions, we are affected. Our vibrations, our frequency, shifts toward that of the external sound. Composers of film scores, for example, entrain audiences to tense in fearful anticipation when the sinister music begins, or swell with emotion when the strings begin to play a romantic theme.

We do have some choice over the effect of entrainment. The more we open and give ourselves to the experience of listening to music, the greater its impact. Although background music is wonderful for creating an ambient mood, placing our full focus on a piece of music provides a wider palette of possibilities. This is the difference between the physical act of "hearing," which is a passive experience, and "listening," which requires our participation. We are also more likely to experience the full power of music when the volume is high enough to command our attention, rather than the music being so soft that it has to compete with background noises. And when we close our eyes, the impact of music is even further heightened—the competing stimuli of external sights is taken away, and the music tends to evoke greater and more vivid imagery out of our own imagination.

In opening ourselves to entrainment, we not only hear the long, slowly rising violin melody of Ralph Vaughan Williams's "The Lark Ascending"—our heart also takes wings and flies. We hear the pounding, primitive rhythms of Igor Stravinsky's "The Rites of Spring," and soon we are throbbing with intensity and passion. (At the first public performance of this piece, the audience rioted, although there is some debate as to whether this was due to the entrainment of the listeners into an atavistic frenzy, or their rage at Stravinsky's iconoclastic breaking of contemporary musical conventions.) If we really listen to the timeless (literally—without a steady beat) melodic lines and elongated vowel tones of Gregorian chant, the unison male voices drifting toward the heavens in the long acoustic reverberation of the cathedral, our bodies effortlessly begin slowing down while our soul gently rises heavenward.

Healers of all kinds draw on this evocative power of music. Many well-known consciousness seminars and trainings rely heavily on music to help open participants to deeper levels of experience. Music is an integral part of healing modalities such as breath work and rebirthing. Combined with guided imagery and body work, songs like "The Rose" or "Bridge Over Troubled Water" trigger deep wells of repressed emotion, even in people hearing these pieces for the first time. Profound experiences of deep nurturing and healing are evoked by singing lullabies to people while being gently rocked and cradled. Recordings of chant played to individuals in these altered states often elicit experiences of oneness, of being touched by a Divine presence.

The Power of the Breath

It all begins with the breath — our voice . . . chant . . . and life itself. We can live without water for weeks, food for months or more, but we cannot live without breath for more than just a few minutes. Breath is the immediate, palpable projection of our life force into the world. Zen master Thich Nhat Hanh called breath "the bridge which connects life to consciousness." Sufi master Hazrat Inayat Khan says that "life's mystery lies in the breath."

In Western traditions, the words for "breath" and "soul" are intimately related. The Greek word *psyche* (meaning "soul") comes from the same root as *psychein,* which means "to breathe." In Hebrew, the word for breath, *ruach,* means "Spirit," while in Latin, the words for "soul" (*anima*) and "Spirit" (*animus*) both derive from the word for "wind" (*anemos*).

Vocal sound is essentially audible breath, and in the sacred sounds of chanting, we begin — and end — with the breath. We breathe deeply, for we need robust columns of vibrating air to support the chant. But we also breathe deeply in chanting because breath is itself the very *ruach,* "life's mystery," the gateway between earth and heaven.

> "Tell me, what is God?
> He is the breath inside the breath."
> —*Kabir*

In claiming the power of chant for ourselves, we also need to reclaim our breath. As young children, we naturally took slow, deep breaths, but between our sedentary lifestyles, a lifetime of inhibiting the spontaneous expression of emotions, and the chronic stress with which most of us live, we tend to breathe very shallowly. Drawing air primarily into the upper portion of our lungs—in the chest—we breathe, on average, twelve to fourteen times a minute. Extensive medical research has proven that many health benefits result from breathing slowly and deeply into the diaphragm—about six breaths a minute is optimal. In my studies of meditation and mysticism, teachers have consistently emphasized the importance of increasing our awareness of the breath. Just by changing our breathing, we can change almost instantly how we feel. Deep, full, diaphragmatic breathing is an easy and powerful way to calm the mind and help heal the body.

As part of learning to chant, you will be taught this style of breathing in chapter 5. But the experience of chanting itself, without any prior training, alters how we breathe. The long phrases of many styles of chant encourage us to draw the breath out, so that our breathing naturally becomes deeper. As the musical phrases of chant repeat, so do the few pauses where there is space to breathe. Our rate of breathing begins to lock in with the repetitive rhythm of the chant, and our breath is naturally channeled into rhythmic patterns similar to the consciousness-altering breathing practices taught by many mystical traditions. When we chant in a group, we also breathe together in the same musical pauses, creating a unified field of breath and laying the foundation for the experience of the communion of sound.

The Power of Sonic Effects

While all music has the power to anchor and entrain, vocal sounds have some special properties, many of which are especially pronounced in chant, that directly impact our consciousness. These are: vocal expression, toning, harmonics, and mantra.

Vocal expression

Long before there was language, our ancestors' voices spontaneously sounded their declarations of anger, fear, love, and joy. While language has to a degree supplanted these immediate, emotional vocalizations, occasionally we still burst forth in preverbal expression. "Mmmmmm," we instinctively intone, savoring the first bite of a delicious meal. "Ahhhh," we exclaim in experiencing the first waves of pleasurable sensations. We release great emotional energy through nonverbal vocal sounds—moaning in pain and sighing with relief. Our family's recent whitewater raft trip down the Green River in Utah was accompanied by screams of excitement, peals of tension-relieving laughter, shouts of triumph, and a few shrieks of terror as we flipped over in the aptly named Disaster Falls.

Practice making a few of these nonverbal noises we all use in communicating raw energy and feeling. Try gasping out loud in surprise. What is the growling sound you make when really annoyed? What about groaning in dismay? Make the sound of "Shhhhh" to silence those around you. And end by laughing for a good ten seconds, in this universal vocalization of happiness.

Language has not replaced tone—it rests on top of the expressive inflections of voice. This is most obvious in the Chinese family of languages which use singsong variations of tone to distinguish different meanings of characters and words that on paper look exactly the same. In Pekinese, the word *yi* represents 215 distinct possibilities, depending on the rising and falling pitches of the speaker. Be especially careful when speaking Cantonese, as the word for "yes"—*hae*—with only a slight variation in pitch also stands for the female sexual organs.

But even in English we communicate as much through our tone of voice as we do through words. "That's great!" can mean how delighted I am, but with a different tone it expresses frustration at some unpleasant event. "Get out of here!" could be a strong request for someone to leave, or a jovial response of disbelief to a friend's surprising statement. In my work over the years as a helping professional, I have learned to listen as much to the tone of what people say as to the content of their words. The words we speak conceal and confuse as much as they communicate, but our voice unfailingly expresses a rich world of feeling and nuance to those who know how to hear this inner music.

Our spontaneous sounds are one of the ways we express emotion, discharge energy, and bring our body and psyche back into balance. When we sigh with relief, we are letting go of built-up anxiety or tension. The experience of making love is heightened by the exotic range of preverbal sounds exchanged by lovers. In times of overwhelming grief such as the death of a loved one, people all over the world keen, letting out loud, sobbing moans and mournful cries, letting the sounds of grief wash through us.

Part of chant's effect lies simply in the reality that for as long as we are chanting, we are vocalizing. We are continually moving energy within our body and our psyche, and expressing it outward as sound.

Toning

Toning is the intentional utterance of an elongated vowel sound; and it is the vocal foundation of chant. The practice of toning consciously and purposefully uses such sounds for healing and spiritual development. Regular toning is excellent for expanding breathing capacity. During a workshop with the well-known toning researcher and musician Karolyn van Putten, one elderly man suffering from Parkinson's disease told the group that toning—recommended to him by a speech therapist to improve his speaking ability—had increased his lung capacity by more than 100 percent. The health benefits we've already cited for chant—lowered blood pressure, pain relief, and so on—all hold true for toning.

Because of the extended length of time we hold vowels in toning, we create especially strong internal vibrations of sound that wash through our organs and bones, stimulate the frontal lobes of the brain, and touch every cell of the body. In many non-Western traditions, Zen for example, toning is believed to reestablish the original resonance of different organs. Working within the Indian system of mind/body healing, many toning practitioners use extended vowel sounds to cleanse the *chakras* (the wheel-like vortices of life energy that interpenetrate the physical body) and rebalance the body's energy systems. Specific vowel sounds are believed by some to have particular resonance with certain organs or chakras. The sound "Ah," for instance, is usually associated with the heart chakra.

It is easy to demonstrate that certain vowels physically vibrate in different parts of our body. Place one hand on your chest. Rest the fingertips of your other hand lightly on your throat. Now, sing the syllable "Ahhhhh" in a strong, full voice. Feel how your chest vibrates with sound? Now, while continuing to sing the same musical note, change the vowel to "Eeeee." Notice how the vibrations diminish in the chest but increase in the throat.

We call toning the foundation of chant, because chant so often makes such powerful use of the extended vowel sounds characteristic of toning. The Sufis chant "Allahhhhh," Christians intone "Ahhhhh-men," while the famous Sanskrit "Ommmmm" has been embraced by a number of traditions. Gregorian chant is based on elongated vowel tones, drawn out across many notes in long musical phrases called *melismas*. Chant affects our physiology and our mind through this capacity of vocal tones to vibrate inside our body with massagelike effects.

Harmonics: The "light in music"

When you play the note middle C on the piano, a felt-tipped hammer strikes a wound metal string, causing it to vibrate at a particular frequency—in this case, 256 vibrations per second. This vibrating string produces a sound called the *fundamental tone*. The sound waves of the fundamental tone not only set other strings and the piano's sound board resonating, but a collection of other higher tones called *harmonics* or *overtones* are triggered and begin vibrating.

It is the combination of the fundamental tone *and* the overtones together, that our ear hears as middle C. Harmonics (along with resonance) give the fundamental tones of various instruments or voices their timbre (pronounced tam-ber), or musical color. Harmonics are what make the sound of the flute pure and clear or that of the cello so warm.

The Greek mathematician Pythagoras, observing that planets are separated by intervals that correspond precisely to the harmonic lengths of strings, looked to music to understand the ultimate principles of proportion, order, and harmony in the universe, which he believed found ultimate expression in the *"music of the spheres."* Mystics throughout history have been fascinated by harmonics, which occur according to a precise mathematical series of whole-number ratios. Many traditions believe that the harmonics in sound are the source of its healing and spiritual power, and some refer to these overtones as "the light in music."

Many varieties of chant strongly emphasize the intentional production of harmonics through toning. When I first heard Tibetan overtone chanting on recordings from the Gyuto and Gyume Monasteries, despite the liner notes, I found it impossible to believe that the monks were singing only one note, as my trained musical ear heard quite clearly a chord of several distinct notes, along with occasional ghostly shimmers of high whistles and other tones of unknown origin. This style of chanting, with its rich and highly developed overtones, is said to be an embodiment of the fully developed speech of the Buddha and is attributed with powers to heal and raise consciousness.

Based on a traditional style of throat singing called *hoomi*, from the Tuvic region of Mongolia, many contemporary chanters have learned to produce two distinct pitch lines: the fundamental note which is sustained as a drone; while simultaneously singing a piercing, whistling melody line of overtones. It was these high overtones that triggered the mind-bending experience of our young engineer in the sound truck while I was toning.

The research of Dr. Tomatis and others suggests that it is particularly these high-frequency harmonics in sacred chant that neuroelectrically charge the brain and heal the body.

Mantra

As we discovered in chapter 2, most spiritual traditions believe that the Creation was a manifestation of sacred sound. Their mystical sects, which seek to give devotees direct access to the Godhead, all teach practices built on the uttering of certain sacred sounds. In the Kabbalah, the mystical sect of Judaism, while the actual name of G-d is considered too holy to be spoken, great attention and practice is devoted to the study and pronunciation of mystical letters. Sufis have their *wazifa* and Hindus their *mantram*—words, according to Sufi Master Hazrat Inayat Khan, that have mystical power to "work upon each atom of the body, making it sonorous, making it a medium of communication between the external life and the inner life." The mysticism of sound has been evolved to a high level of sophistication in these traditions, with ninety-nine *wazifas* and countless mantras each designed to produce particular effects when chanted. In some practices, mantras are customized according to the characteristics and needs of the devotee. In other traditions, mantras are handed from teacher to disciple, and carry within them *baraka* or *shaktipat*—the spiritual force transmitted by the teacher.

The theories of pioneering philosopher and biochemist Rupert Sheldrake would suggest that ancient chants have been infused with power and meaning from the voices and devotion of millions of people over centuries, creating a kind of energy field (called a morphic field) that impacts us here today as we intone the sacred syllables. Whatever the reason, practitioners of mantric chanting are usually convinced as a result of their own experience that these particular syllables and sounds do have extraordinary power.

The Power of Intent

If my eighty-five-year-old grandmother was chanting the name of a Native American tribe by mistake, how do we account for the seemingly positive results she experienced? While some teachers of mantra insist that the exact words and pronunciation are critical, others like the well-respected Swami Sivananda tell us that "Your sincerity and what is in your heart and mind are more important than the pronunciation." Swami Muktananda, the meditation master who brought the well-known Siddha yoga to the West, says "Only if the goal of mantra is present in your mind will it bear fruit."

While chant affects us through anchoring, entrainment, and sonic effects even without our conscious participation, it is when the power of our intent, our desire, and our will are united with these intrinsic powers that chant realizes its full transformational potential. Rabbi Zalman Schachter-Shalomi, founder of the Jewish Renewal Movement, said to me that "The power of chant all has to do with *covanai*—conscious intent. To whom am I chanting? And for what?"

When we give ourselves to chanting—heart, mind, and body— when we passionately desire to discover Spirit in sound, then we have created the ideal conditions for chant to blossom and bring its sweet nectar into our lives.

Chapter Four

Common Threads:
Chant Around the World

"Flowers and bees may be different, but the honey is the same.
Systems of faith may be different, but God is One."
—Rig Veda

The little Chapel of Saint Joseph at the National Cathedral in Washington, D.C., offers refreshing sanctuary from the sweltering hot July evening; the granite walls are smooth and cool to the touch. In the center of this round vault, some sixty people are sitting in a circle chanting in Latin over and over again, *"Veni, Sancte Spiritus,"* — "Come, Holy Spirit." Part of the dynamic movement known as Taizé, ecumenical groups of Protestants and Catholics all over the world, especially young people, gather for services completely of chant. Everyone sings, facilitated by long repetitions of simple lines of music and some lyrics in the vernacular. "Come, Holy Spirit." The sound of the voices echoes and reverberates through the room. "Come, Holy Spirit." The energy builds slowly, deliberately. High harmonics shimmer like crystal icicles in the high ceilings. Simple words, bottomless words, undulating in repeating cycles of prayer. In the magic of chant and in the deep silence that follows, the palpable sense of Holy Spirit resonates throughout the chapel.

The old Jewish hotel in the Catskill Mountains of New York has been transformed into a beautiful spiritual oasis for the study and practice of Siddha yoga, a traditional Indian lineage popular in the West. Well over a thousand mostly middle-class devotees are chanting in the former main ballroom facing the empty chair reserved for their teacher, called Gurumai. In the air, a taste of the distinctive aroma of sandalwood incense; the lights in the cut-glass chandeliers are dimmed, creating a soft ambiance. A small group of first-rate musicians play the tamboura, harmonium, and mridangam, while the leader and audience call and respond the traditional Sanskrit chanting of names of the Divine: *"Krishna govinda, govinda, go pala."* Beginning slowly, over the course of thirty minutes the tempo picks up, faster and faster, hands start to clap, bodies sway, building to an ecstatic crescendo of sound and Spirit.

It's a warm fall afternoon in one of the old mining towns in the hills above Denver. Several hundred people are gathered inside the regional high-school gym—Native Americans in the traditional dress of a dozen tribes or ubiquitous T-shirts and jeans; equal numbers of Caucasians, some sporting turquoise necklaces, concha belts, or feathers tied in their hair; local shoppers sampling the crafts, while others are feeding their spiritual hunger. The powwow is filled with the smells of corn dogs and fried dough, and pulsing with the sounds of chant. A group of six males, ranging from young boys to a grandfather, beat together on the huge bass drum sitting in the center of their circle, singing the traditional songs and chants of their people. Some folks are dancing the "fancy shawl," others cluster around the singers, while still others drift around the gym, talking, laughing, listening . . . all entrained to the heartlike beat.

One of the benefits of our shrinking globe is the incredible richness of cultural cross-pollination: Thai food in small-town shopping malls, immigrants selling traditional African woodcarvings out of suitcases on big city streets, hand-knit alpaca Peruvian hats hanging from wooden carts in airport concourses—and chant.

Until recently, to find recorded chant (other than Gregorian) one had to search through obscure catalogs or libraries of ethnomusicology. Today, with a quick telephone call, computer linkup, or trip to your local store, you can easily fill your home and car with the spiritual music of Senegal, Siberia, and Sumatra, ancient Hebrew chants, or contemporary Christian spirituals. And you do not have to travel to the Zen temples in Kyoto to join in Buddhist chanting, nor journey to Rumi's tomb in Konya, Turkey, to chant the traditional *zhikrs*. Almost anywhere you may live, there are opportunities to share firsthand with other seekers the beauty and Spirit of live chanting. More and more people are rediscovering the joy of chant in their own traditions, while experiencing the spiritually charged sound vibrations of other cultures.

My early involvement with the Sufi Order of the West fostered my own ecumenical approach to chanting. Gathering every Sunday night in a Cambridge church basement, a spontaneous altar was created in the center of the room. Small devotional candles in colored glass holders surrounded photographs of Hindu saints, paintings of Jesus and Saint Francis, pictures of Sufi masters and Native American shamans, and a Jewish menorah. We always opened with the invocation that begins, "Toward the One . . ."—meaning the One that is at the heart of every faith and every path. This Sufi order, though born out of the mystical heart of Islam, proclaims that the "Sufi sees the same truth in each religion, and therefore regards all as one." Their dances consciously invoke the Divine Presence in all its forms, and so we chanted in Latin and Hebrew, Arabic and Lakota, honoring each tradition while always reaching "toward the One."

Launched on this eclectic path, over the years I've led hymns at born-again churches and chants at High Mass; intoned *Allah hu akbar* in the courtyard of a mosque in Cairo, and *Sh'ma Yisra'el* at the Wailing Wall in Jerusalem; sung Sanskrit *kirtan* for hours, and completely lost track of time chanting in the dark womb of Native American sweat lodges. I've recorded chant masters authentically singing their traditional songs, while also experimenting with new cultural blends. A few years ago, sound healer Jonathan Goldman and I recorded twenty-four tracks of ourselves singing Buddhist-like overtone chanting in the one-time-only performance of the two-member "Tibetan-Jewish-American men's choir."

Despite the many outward differences, there is a core of shared truth that lies at the heart of all spiritual paths: the knowledge of a divine, creative force that permeates all of reality, and the belief that something of that divine nature lives within each of us. These simple truths have found expression in a wondrous diversity of religions, sects, philosophies, tribal cultures, and spiritual paths. The One Spirit has been invoked as God, Goddess, Adonai, Brahma, Allah, Yemaya, Wakan Tanka—a thousand honored names—by worshipers, devotees, the *kehilah, chelas,* and *mureeds.* We recognize the divine spark within us as soul, Atman, Buddha nature, *neshamah,* the Self, or among the Semong pygmies, Kemuit.

"Every religion," says religious scholar Huston Smith, "is a blend of universal principles and local setting." This idea, commonly referred to as the "Perennial Philosophy," emphasizes the common mystical core of all spiritual traditions. Author and Roman Catholic monk Bede Griffiths describes the world's religions as being like fingers on a hand. If we look at each finger separately, it appears unique and apart. But if we follow it down to its roots, we then see that the fingers all come from the same hand.

Of course, while some speak of the One Spirit that permeates all forms, others are passionate about the superiority of their own. Bede's own experiments in communal worship took place in India, the subcontinent that birthed the universal heart of Gandhi, but also spawned bloody wars between Hindu and Moslem. It is a bitter irony that the question of how best to honor the Creator has led to religious conflicts lasting centuries—between Christians and Muslims, Jews and Christians, even Protestants and Catholics.

It is the mystical branches of each religion, those which espouse the direct experience of God without the need for intercession by a priestly caste, that tend to most understand and embrace the perspective of Gandhi: "Religions are different roads converging to the same point. What does it matter that we take different roads, so long as we reach the same goal? . . . In God's house there are many mansions, and they are equally holy."

It is no wonder that chant has the power to find common ground between spiritual paths and that the chant of other traditions can move us so deeply. For chant offers us the direct experience of what we read in the religious texts. If we give ourselves to the journey, chant helps take us beyond concepts, beyond philosophy, beyond forms. Chant is a doorway to the Divine. Whatever the mode, the rhythm or tune, by whatever name holiness is invoked, in the living, breathing vibration of chant—there is God.

For those who seek a deep life of Spirit, there are advantages to giving oneself fully to a single path. Spiritual teachers of all faiths warn us of the supermarket approach—"I think I'll try a little Buddhist meditation. . . . Oh, that's too hard, I like the guided meditation tapes better. . . . Gee, my friends are all doing yoga. . . . I really should reread the Bible—maybe the abridged edition?"

Yet many committed seekers who stand rooted in their own religion have benefited from exposure to the chants of other paths. Episcopal priest Cynthia Snodgrass finds that Sanskrit chanting has really deepened her understanding of church ritual in her own tradition. "The rituals in which the Sanskrit was chanted—like those found in the *Rig Veda*—go so much further back than those of my own faith. Sanskrit chanting has never been a barrier to my Christian worship—as a matter of fact, I find that it deepens it."

While there is a resonant core of Spirit within all mystical traditions, there are also important differences in their paths, practices, and philosophies. I believe that it is vitally important not to minimize these differences, nor seek to homogenize the beautiful diversity of spiritual life. Every spiritual tradition has come up with its own answers to universal questions, and their uniqueness is expressed and celebrated in their chant.

Hindu Chant

Daybreak. On the banks of the sacred Ganges River a crowd is drawn to the clanging of bells from the small stone temple. In the foothills of the Himalayas, a wandering *sadhu,* forehead smeared with ash and dressed in orange robes, stands to greet the dawn. In urban ashrams in Los Angeles and Berlin, São Paulo and Capetown, Indian expatriates and Western devotees stop in on their way to work to share in the morning ritual. Traditionally chanted at dawn as a meditation on the brilliant splendor of the sun—symbolizing the light of creation—each morning, millions of voices intone the deep rhythms of the *Gaayatri mantra:*

> "Om Bhoor Bhuvassuvah
> Om Tat Saviturvarenyam

Bhargo Devasya Dheemahi
Dhiyo Yo Nah Prachodayaat."

"May there be peace on mortal, immortal, and Divine planes.
I meditate on the most brilliant splendor of the divine sun.
May He stimulate our intellect,
So that we are inspired to take the right action at the right time."

An ancient religion originating in India over three thousand years ago, Hinduism believes there is a unified ultimate reality, called Brahman. Westerners are sometimes bewildered by the enormous array of Hindu deities: Blue-skinned Krishna, playing his flute and making love to the ten thousand milkmaids; Ganesh, god of the household with the head of an elephant; Kali, the Dark Mother who eats our karma, often seen in a ferocious pose wearing a garland of skulls; the resourceful and clever trickster Hanuman, the monkey god, the paragon of loyalty and devotion. Yet beneath the many faces and forms, Hinduism sees only one Divinity that lives in all of creation. And this Divinity lives within us as well, a divine soul, the *Atman,* our own Inner Self. The traditional Hindu greeting is the *namaskar,* bowing with the hands palm to palm in front of the forehead: "I honor in you that which is Divine."

"God is in truth the whole universe: what was, what is, and what beyond shall ever be . . .
He is the inmost soul of all, which like a little flame the size of a thumb is hidden in the hearts of men."

—*Svetasvatara Upanishad*

Within Hinduism, there exists a variety of paths or yogas, among them: Jnana yoga, the path of wisdom; Bhakti yoga, the path of devotion; Karma yoga, the path of selfless service; Raja yoga, the "kingly" path. All forms of yoga make use of chant. The word *yoga* means "yoke" or union with God, and the purpose of all these practices and Sanskrit chanting is just that—for us to know and experience our own divine nature, the *Atman,* to become one with God.

While Hinduism remains a vital living tradition for hundreds of millions of Indians, this ancient spiritual wisdom has also found a welcome home in the West. The past decades have witnessed a tremendous proliferation of the psychophysical forms of Hatha yoga, flowing from the backwaters of once-obscure ashrams into the mainstream of Western life—appearing in health clubs, YMCAs, hospitals, and on television. Taught by organizations ranging from TM (Transcendental Meditation) to stress-management clinics, many millions of westerners chant Sanskrit mantras every day. This marriage of the ancient and modern is symbolized in a global satellite chanting network, where many thousands of people on three continents use the latest communications technology to join together in chanting the names of God.

Of all the traditions we will visit, there is none in which chant plays a more central role than Hindu/Vedic culture. The importance of chant is firmly rooted in their belief that sound vibration is the basic nature of the universe—*Nada Brahman*—sound is God. According to the sacred scriptures, the Upanishads, the cosmos was created out of the primal ethers through the uttering of the primal sound—*shabda*—embodied in the sacred syllable "OM":

"The word OM is the imperishable; all this its manifestation.
Past, present, future—everything is OM."
—*Mandukya Upanishad*

The Sanskrit language is essentially a three-thousand-year-old science of sound, composed of "sounds and words based on the subtle vibrations that underlie the elements of the world," says Swami Akandananda of the SYDA Yoga Foundation in South Fallsburg, New York. "There is an inherent connection between the sound of Sanskrit and the actual reality that it represents."

Especially potent syllables, called *bija* or seed syllables, are strung together like genes on a strand of DNA to form chants called *mantram* (meaning in Sanskrit an "instrument of thought"). The *bijas* themselves—for example, *Om, Aim, Hrim, Shim,* or *Glim*—have no literal meaning, but are interspersed with actual words as in the following mantra invoking the power of Ganesh, remover of obstacles:

> "Om Aim Hrim Shim Glim Glaum Ham Ganapataye
> Varavarada Sarva Jana Me Vasamanaya Svaha."

A mantra is more than just a prayer. As author Deepak Chopra once told me, "They are literally holograms of information and energy." When we chant the sacred mantras, we are transformed and awakened to higher states of consciousness by the very nature and power of the sounds. Well-known Sanskrit scholar Dr. Vyaas Houston describes listening to his teacher intone the ancient texts: "When he chanted, it was as though every molecule of his body was vibrating. It felt as if the entire universe dissolved into a state of vibration."

> "My body caught fire like an ember
> as I brought the syllable OM,
> the one that says You are That,
> into me."
> —*Poems of Lalla* (trans. Coleman Barks)

Not only do Indian chants have potent "lyrics," but the music itself is consciously designed to affect our state of being. Indian music is based on *ragas*, melodic patterns arising out of their traditional musical scales. Each raga is associated with specific moods such as *adbhuta* (wonderment) or *karuna* (sadness). Some are related to the time of the day (for instance, there are morning or evening ragas), or the cycle of the year (such as the rainy season). Specific ragas are also believed to have particular healing or spiritual powers. Ravi Shankar in his autobiography, *My Music, My Life*, tells of traditional stories about the powers of great musicians to perform "miracles by singing certain ragas. It is said that some could light fires or oil lamps by singing one raga, or bring rain, melt stones, cause flowers to bloom, and attract wild animals—even snakes and tigers—to a peaceful, quiet circle in a forest around a singing musician. To us, in this modern, mechanical, materialistic age, all this seems like a collection of fables, but I sincerely believe that these stories are all true."

Whatever you may believe about the inherent power of bijas, mantras, and ragas, like many other westerners in recent years, I have experienced again and again the awesome power of Hindu chanting. My most ecstatic experiences of chant have been doing *kirtan* (Indian devotional chanting) intoning *Shri Ram Jai Ram* or *Om Namaha Shivaya*, singing the names of God, faster and faster, the inner fire of *kundalini* rising, my heart and soul lifted into a state that could only be described as *ananda*—bliss.

Christian Chant

The work day begins in New England. Cars stream down busy expressways and squeeze into jammed parking lots, crowded elevators unload their human cargo to pour into offices buzzing with the sounds of computers and copy machines, the jangling of telephones, and a cacophony of voices.

Just off Route 155 in rural Vermont, the Benedictine monks of the

Weston Priory are silently gathering for the third time today—to chant. They began this day, like every other, at 5 A.M. in the womb-like darkness of the unlit oratory, chanting the fifteen-hundred-year-old prayers of *Vigils:* "I will say to the darkness, 'be my light.'" Later, as dawn broke over the tree-clad Green Mountains, they chanted psalms of praise in the service called *Lauds:*

"O sing unto the Lord a new song . . .
Break forth and sing for joy, yea sing praises."

Now, as commuters enter their offices, the brothers begin the third of the eight monastic daily intervals or "canonical hours" called *Prime.* Each of the eight sacred hours has its *office,* or service, filled with chants that evoke the virtues appropriate to the unique natural and spiritual qualities of that period of day or night. Chanting, "The sun has risen, the sun has risen," the brothers prepare to work. When the strains of the last "Amen" fade into stillness, they will exchange their gray tunics and black scapulars for blue jeans and flannel shirts as they tend their gardens, chop wood, make pottery, and create silver and enamel jewelry. During the three "little hours" of the day— *Terce* at midmorning, *Sext* at noon, and *None* during late afternoon— they will put down their hoes and stop their potter's wheel, and kneel to privately chant a psalm.

Just after 5 P.M., these Benedictine monks, like their brothers and sisters around the world, will assemble for *vespers*—the Lighting of the Lamp—and again at 8 P.M. for *Compline*—"Completion"—the end of their monastic day. As light gives way to darkness, they intone:

"Salve regina, mater misericordiae . . ."
"Hail Mary, we greet thee, Mother and Queen all merciful:
Our life, our sweetness, and our hope."

The day ends, as it began, with chant. Then the monks return silently to their rooms.

Christians, part of the world's largest organized religion, worship Jesus Christ as the incarnate Son of God. While all Christians share this belief in the divinity of Jesus and hold as sacred texts the Old and New Testaments of the Holy Bible, there is a wide and complex range of doctrines, liturgies, and rituals expressed through three main branches: Roman Catholic, Eastern Orthodox, and the many denominations of Protestant. Early in Christian history, Saint Augustine declared that, "To sing is to pray twice," and sung prayer has been central to all its denominations. Chant wears many faces in Christendom: from Gregorian chant to the African drums and rhythms of the monks of Keur Moussa in Senegal; from stately Lutheran hymns to gospel.

Among these practices, Gregorian chant is unique in providing an unbroken link not only to the sung prayers of early Christians, but back more than three thousand years to the Jewish tradition of chanting sacred texts, especially the psalms. It is most likely that these early chants were augmented speech—with the words mostly sung on one note, perhaps with a neighboring note to begin and end a chant. As Christian chant evolved, so did its musical range, developing melody and the characteristic extended flow of notes on a single vowel sound called *melismas*.

Father Theophane, chant master of the Snowmass Benedictine Monastery in Colorado, talked to me about his experience of Gregorian chant: "It is a whole world which is home—reassuring, warm, sacred. When we chant, I feel connected to centuries of monks who have chanted in just this way. It is a real prayer and a sacrament of unity for all of us living here."

Gregorian chant is named after Gregory I, the Roman Catholic

Pope who in the late sixth century ordained that these liturgical chants be collected and preserved. He is often pictured with a dove—the symbol of the Holy Spirit—whispering the sacred words and sounds into his ear. Called *plainsong* because of its musically unadorned style, Gregorian chant (as well as the related chant forms of Old Roman, Byzantine, Ambrosian, and Coptic) always consists of a single melody line. In contrast to Sanskrit chant where the actual sound vibrations of the chant are paramount, in Christian chant it is the text and its meaning that lies at the heart of the practice. There is relatively little of the repetition we see in mantric practices—the music moves on like an endless stream following the flow of the text. With no harmony, no instrumental accompaniment—not even a meter or rhythm—Gregorian chant breathes mystical life into the psalms, hymns, and prayers that make up the more than three thousand individual chants. Traditionally sung in stone chapels, monasteries, and cathedrals with high ceilings, Gregorian chant has a numinous, timeless quality as the elongated vowels reverberate into eternity.

Like all Catholic worship, Gregorian chants were historically performed in Latin or occasionally Greek; but since the mid-sixties, Catholic services and chanting are increasingly performed in the vernacular. The impact of chant extends far beyond the monasteries and convents. A 1993 recording of traditional Gregorian chant by the Benedictine monks of the Spanish monastery of Santo Domingo de Silos has sold more than five million copies around the world. The monks of Weston Priory have a singing ministry, and their many recordings of folk-style liturgical songs and chants in English have opened the hearts of ecumenical audiences for decades. The primary form for Catholic worship, the Mass, sometimes incorporates a style of chant called litany, where the congregation responds to text chanted by the priest with a simple repeated sung phrase such as *"Ora pro nobis*—Lord hear our prayer." And as part of a worldwide effort to revive dwindling church attendance, especially among young people, movements like the Charismatic Catholics and Taizé rely on participatory chant to provide everyone the direct experience of Spirit in sound that has been the daily domain of monks and nuns.

In the New Testament, Paul instructs the Ephesians to "Sing and psalmodize to the Lord with your heart and for everything giving thanks in the name of our Lord Jesus Christ to God the Father." If you walked in the door of the Apostolic House of Prayer just outside of Norfolk, Virginia, you would hear the congregation faithfully following Saint Paul's instructions by singing the same Psalms as the Benedictines. But instead of the lilting lines of Gregorian, your body would be immediately lifted up in a sea of rhythm. The drummer lays into the back beat with the thump-thump of the electric bass, while the Hammond organ, digital piano, and electric guitar trade funky riffs. The choir—dressed in identical red robes with purple trim—are up out of their seats, swaying left and right, hands clapping, leading the mostly black congregation in chanting praise to Jesus in the words of the Ninety-sixth Psalm. "Sing to the Lord a new song." "Yeah, yeah, yeah, yeah, Je-sus," a soprano woman's voice belts out over the choir. "Yeah, yeah, Jesus." The choir responds in vibrant four-part harmony, "Sing to the Lord a new song; Sing to the Lord all the earth. Sing to the Lord, praise His name."

While some might not consider this kind of gospel singing to be chanting, its high degree of participation, repetition of phrases, and overt evocation of Spirit places it firmly in our study of the world of chant.

The music grows to a fevered crescendo of feeling and sound, as men and women openly weep, several fall out on the floor—overwhelmed with Spirit and joy. "Jesus is here in this music," one older man tells me. "I can feel his loving self right here in this church, and I want him to know how much I love him."

This gospel service started at nine o'clock this Sunday morning and—with a short break for a late lunch and socializing—will continue until well after dinnertime. Music and chant make Spirit a living experience. "Sing to the Lord, praise His name!" Finally, as night falls, everyone chants the words to Psalm 124:

"May the Lord, maker of heaven and earth,
bless you from Zion."

Many miles to the north, as the same sun sets on their monastery, the monks are intoning their Compline hymn in the traditional style of Gregorian chant. And as the lights are extinguished, their voices sound out, a refined echo of their fundamentalist brothers and sisters:

"May the Lord, maker of heaven and earth,
bless you from Zion."

African Chant

The driving polyrhythms of the drums fill the steamy afternoon with a throbbing heartbeat of sound. The master percussionists "sing" chant patterns on their two-headed talking drums, joined by *shakere* and *agbe* calabash drums and metal bells in a complex pulsing tapestry of rhythm. Chanting voices cry out *"Omode koni'ko sh'iba 'go!* — Make way, I pay homage to the Owner of vital force!" — as bodies begin swaying and feet start to move. In this Nigerian village, the festival's procession has begun with the invocation of Elleggua — deity of the crossroads and a notorious trickster. Next come farmers, dancing and chanting a specialized chant form known as *ijala* with their appeal for fertile fields and much-needed rain. The hunters are next, seeking blessings and good fortune for the hunt from Ogun,

Spirit guardian of iron. Each group—every occupation—chants the words and melodies unique to their guilds, their voices an ecstatic play of call and response. *"Ode t'o t'ode ni i-lera lojun ina"*—"It's only the best hunters who have bush meat roasting before their kitchen fire"—sings out a chant leader. *"L'a a wa forin Ogun naa si I*—"We burst into songs pleasing to Ogun"—comes the reply.

They chant to the *Orishas*—divine beings representing God's power on earth—each deity invoked by properly consecrated drums and special percussive patterns that take years to master. They sing praises to Shango, who rules over thunder and lightning, to invoke his boldness and fire—accompanied by the *bata,* a cone-shaped drum. They chant to Yemaya—goddess of the sea and moon, said to be "greater than the oceans and more nurturing than their waters": *"Yemaya Asesu, Asesu Yemaya. Yemaya a lodo, a lodo Yemaya . . ."* Before the procession is over, they will call out to Obatala, named King of the White Cloth for his purity and honesty; Orunmila, the deity of wisdom and divination; the terrifying female warrior, Oya; and the all-powerful Oloddumare.

While the chants have been orally passed down from generation to generation since the dawn of history, individuals are also free to improvise and express their own unique style and personality in calling to the others, for play and spontaneity are honored in this tradition. There are many more *Orishas* to invite to this gathering, and the dancing and chanting continue all day. The chanting voices merge, then separate; the syncopated rhythms, dancing off each other, circle in a melange of continually shifting musical textures. And always—the pounding drums that stir up dust and Spirit in this west African village.

It is difficult to speak of an "African" tradition of chant, for the continent contains over thirty separate major language groups and many hundreds of tribal or ethnic groups, each with its own music and traditions. African chant includes the haunting polyphony of the Iruti forest pygmies, the beautiful harmonies of the Zulu hymns, and the ancient Coptic chants of Ethiopia. But there are some elements common to most chants throughout sub-Saharan Africa.

Drumming uplifts the Spirit of African chant on a tide of rhythm more sophisticated than almost anywhere else in the world. Drums are often consecrated to a specific *Orisha* and used only for particular rituals. Among the Banyankele people, drums even "live" in their own sacred huts, have their own herds of cattle, and are offered milk daily. The traditional African nonlinear sense of time is reflected in chant forms that are cyclic and improvisational, the chant flowing like a river as the interlocking polyrhythms of the drums pulse and shift and circle.

And where there are drums playing, bodies start to move. Author and Yoruba ceremonialist Luisah Teish emphasizes the sharp contrast between her tradition and those where chant is a contemplative, inward journey or takes us out of the body. "Our chant is very, very embodied—people always feeling and expressing the Spirit of the music by moving and dancing."

African chant is also a deeply communal experience. According to anthropologist, musician, and Yoruba initiate George Brandon, "Chanting is always done by groups of people—it's very rare, if ever, that it would be done alone. In fact, musically the forms all require a call and response, or a distribution of pitches among a group. Chant is a part of every aspect of religious and social life throughout the continent. It summons up and creates an energy that people use for a collective purpose."

Chanting brings the community together in sound and Spirit by helping to organize daily activity. There are specific chants for harvesting a field, another for making herbal medicines, still another for fixing a wheel. Lullabies, children's songs, and chants for games and leisure are sung throughout the day. Chant is used to transmit knowledge and spiritual teaching, and to empower the many rituals that mark the stages of life—weddings, births, title-taking ceremonies, and funerals.

In Zimbabwe and other regions, chanting evokes altered states of consciousness used to allow ancestral Spirit possession and for healing. Singing and chanting are used to coordinate the movements of hunters in the brush in pygmy societies of the central rain forest. In Ghana, there are chants for celebrating the loss of a child's first tooth and for teasing bed wetters; among the Yoruba, a special collection of chants are sung by women who deliver twins.

African chanting, like elsewhere, is a living bridge between the physical world and the world of Spirit. Igbo musician and teacher Onye Onyemaechi told me, "Chanting is a way to communicate what we feel to God. In doing this, we are fulfilled in experiencing divine ecstasy, and we are better able to make good decisions about our lives."

African chanting practices, after decades of colonialism, have been influenced by Western music, Christian hymns, and Islam intonations. But the cross-pollination has worked both ways. Yoruba and other traditions migrated with slavery to the New World, giving birth to a host of chant-infused religions such as Santeria, Arara, Xango, and Palo. Many Latin and Afro-Caribbean sounds such as juju music and rhumba arose directly out of traditional African chant and drumming. The gospel singing in the Apostolic House of Prayer, as well as American soul music, jazz, and rhythm and blues, can all trace their musical lineage back to the colors and rhythms of African music and chant. In recent years, the sounds of African chant are increasingly being heard directly by western ears through the recordings of such artists as drumming master Baba Olatunji and Ladysmith Black Mambazo, representing the Zulu male choral style known as *isicathamiya,* with its smooth harmonies and tight vocal blend. Chants to Yemaya have been widely adopted by Western women in honoring the Spirit of the Divine feminine.

In Africa today, wherever traditions run strong, chant is still the heartbeat of communal life, infusing ordinary and extraordinary moments with its pulsing, passionate rhythms. In the words of an ancient Yoruba proverb: "A village without music is a dead place."

Buddhist Chant

The sounds of fluttering prayer flags, whirling prayer wheels, and sacred chant shimmer in the cool, thin air at the roof of the world—the ancient city of Lhasa. Nestled on a small, fertile plain surrounded by the towering Himalayas, for over twelve hundred years this remote Tibetan city has been one of the symbolic centers of Buddhism and the revered destination of millions of pilgrims. Today, inside the Jokhang Temple, the acrid smell of yak butter burning in small silver bowls fills the air, their smoky light adding to the rows of candles in the darkened shrine. Hundreds of pilgrims, long hair wrapped in twin braids tied with colored yarn and dressed in traditional tunics, sit in the cross-legged "lotus position" quietly chanting on a single tone, *"Om Mani Padme Hum."* When intoned with compassion, the six syllables of this powerful Sanskrit mantra—often called "The Diamond in the Lotus"—are said to help purify the suffering of all sentient beings. The pilgrims chant facing an altar that holds a statue of Avalokiteshvara—the beloved Buddha of Compassion.

One hundred miles south in Dharamsala—just over the Indian border—resides His Holiness the fourteenth Dalai Lama, the spiritual and secular leader of Tibet, held by Buddhists to be the living incarnation of Avalokiteshvara. Many thousands of his people cling to their traditions in this tiny mountain town, refugees from the brutal Chinese occupation of their homeland. The great monastic traditions of Tibet are now in disarray due to persecution; monasteries like Drepung Loseling have reestablished themselves in their Indian home-in-exile. Eschewing bitterness, the monks chant for compassion, forgiveness, and peace.

Today, dressed in their ceremonial yellow robes with maroon trim (called *choegoe*) and donning distinctive yellow hats topped with huge crescent-shaped fans, the monks enter the main assembly hall of the monastery and begin chanting to the Buddha in Tibetan the *"Nyen-seng: The Sound of Delight"*:

> "Malu semchen kungi gon syur ching . . ."
> "You are the protector of all sentient beings . . ."

Tibetan monks like those in Drepung produce utterly unique deep-throated vocal tones with such powerful harmonics that each voice is actually sounding three separate notes at the same time. Alternating rhythmic chanting of lines of text with extended vowel tones, the monks intone their "chords" in an otherworldly drone, sharply punctuated with raucous blasts from six-foot curved brass horns (*dungchen*) and the crashes of cymbals (*sil-nyen*). Seated in two rows facing each other, the monks practice visualizations and sacred hand gestures (called *mudras*) while chanting.

Over the course of the ceremony, the monks will chant such prayers as: *"Nyensen*—Invocation of the Forces of Goodness"; *"Tong-nyi*—Sounds of the Void"; and *"Dakzin Tsarchad*—A Melody to Sever the Ego Syndrome." At the end, the monks send forth the smoke of incense to the "ten directions" to "invoke peace in all the world."

Like African chant, the distinctive sound of the Tibetan monks has been increasingly heard by western ears in the past years due to well-distributed recordings, as well as tours by the monks of the Gyuto and Gyume Monasteries, and several Hollywood movies. The overtones that emanate from their voices are an extraordinary phenomenon of sound generating a high level of scientific interest that the monks find bemusing as they do not even have a name for it. Their style of chanting originated many centuries ago when heads of the order had revelations that these sounds would "benefit all human beings." "The most important thing," Tibetan monk Tenzin Dhargye of the Drepung Monastery told me, "is that the chant comes from the heart." In Buddhism, chant is a tool for awakening consciousness, for penetrating the true nature of reality. Surya Das, an American-born lama of the Tibetan Dzogchen lineage, says, "When we chant our hearts open, we lose our finite sense of self, at least momentarily, and encounter our greater Buddha-nature."

The word *Buddha* comes from a Sanskrit word meaning literally "to wake up." This is the central message of Buddhism—that each of us can wake up from the suffering and delusion of everyday existence. Each of us can become a Buddha. The original Buddha was a living man named Siddhartha Gautama, who in the sixth century B.C.E. achieved enlightenment while sitting and meditating under a *bodhi* tree. In his awakening, he discovered an unchanging reality beyond the world of the senses called *nirvana,* which can be realized by a process of dis-identification with our limited ego identity and the cultivation of such qualities as compassion and equanimity. Buddhism is more a highly evolved road map for becoming fully human than about becoming one with the Divine. And while there is an emphasis on achieving personal enlightenment, Buddhism teaches the fundamental importance of working to relieve the suffering of others.

Originating in India, Buddhism shares with Hinduism some use of Sanskrit and the practice of chanting mantram. Buddhism soon migrated to Tibet, Nepal, China, Japan, and southeast Asia, cross-pollinating with local cultures and religious traditions to create today's wide array of lineages and paths. In the eighth century, a Tibetan lama delivered this astonishing prophecy:

"When the Iron Bird flies and horses run of wheel, the Tibetan people will be scattered like ants across the world and the *Dharma* (Sanskrit for "truth" or "the teaching") will come to the land of the red-faced people."

Today, we see this prediction having come to pass in not only the destruction of the Tibetan homeland, but the remarkable growth of Buddhism in the West, especially in the United States.

It is dawn at an urban Zen center on the west coast of "the land of the red-faced people." The rumbling beat of a large standing drum calls people into the main *zendo*. Initially popularized in the United States by Alan Watts, Alan Ginsburg, and others of the "Beat Generation" of the 1950s, this austere Japanese tradition has wide appeal among educated westerners because of its emphasis on sober investigation of the nature of reality through meditation. A less known but important part of Zen practice is its tradition of chanting.

The Zen priest, wearing a black and white robe (called a *kesa*—traditionally made from shrouds of deceased individuals as a reminder of impermanence), offers incense, then bows three full prostrations on the floor. The bell master mindfully "invites" the huge bowl-shaped *keisu* (gong) to sound with a padded stick. As its powerful reverberations resonate in the chests of those gathered, the chanters, sitting cross-legged on black floor cushions, begin intoning the identical ancient Sanskrit words one would hear in Lhasa, Thailand, or Japan:

"Ga-tay, ga-tay, para ga-tay, para sam ga-tay; bodhi svaha."
"Gone. Gone. Gone beyond. Go beyond the beyond.
Hail to the one who awakens."

This chant, called the "Heart of Perfect Wisdom," is said to embody the Buddha's teachings on the illusory nature of reality and the path to awakening from suffering. Punctuated by the sharp "clack-clacks" of a wooden fish-shaped drum, the practitioners intone slowly and rhythmically on a single note, without overt emotion, the English text:

"Form here is only emptiness,
emptiness only form . . ."

While Zen services include extensive chanting of texts in Sanskrit, Japanese, and English, the purpose of Zen chant, according to well-known teacher Roshi Philip Kapleau, is "to sense the reality lying beyond the words, the Emptiness to which they point." Joan Halifax, author and Soto Zen priest, told me "In Zen chanting, the emphasis is not on the words, but on the actual energy coming from the *hara* [Japanese for "belly"]. It's about embodiment and stability—strength of mind and strength of heart." The Zen Peacemaker Order, in which Joan is initiated, ends their evening service with the chant:

"Awaken! Take heed!
Do not squander your life."

There are many faces and many voices of Buddhist chant. Twice each day, twelve million members of the Nichiren Buddhist movement in 128 countries chant in Japanese, "Nam-myoho-renge-kyo," while meditating in front of a sacred scroll called the *Gohonzon*. All the benefits of the Buddha's wisdom contained in the text of the Lotus Sutra are said to be realized by chanting its title: "Nam-myoho-renge-kyo. Nam-myoho-renge-kyo." Meanwhile, in Thailand, hundreds of thousands of russet-robed monks wander forests and towns with their begging bowls to collect food. It is customary for every Thai Buddhist man at least once in his life to shave his head and take vows for periods ranging from weeks to years. In the evenings, you will sometimes see a small cluster of monks sitting under their large umbrellas (called *tudongs*) hung from trees and draped in mosquito netting. As their lit candles illuminate the nets like huge Japanese lanterns, you will hear them chant in Pali for one hour beginning with this invocation to the Buddha:

"Natmo tassa pakhawato arahato samma sampbud tassa."
"I offer respect to you, most high one who has achieved
enlightenment by your own efforts."

A scientist in California is one of millions worldwide who chant "Namo Amitabha Buddha—Homage to the Buddha of boundless light and infinite life." Dedicating his efforts to "the merits of all sentient beings for their rebirth in the pure lands of the Buddha," his daily practice has accumulated 8,426,000 repetitions. "Namo Amitabha Buddha. Namo Amitabha Buddha . . ."

Across all these forms of practice, Buddhist chant is resonant with the tenor of the tradition—slow, meditative, and dispassionate—a far cry from the ecstatic devotional chant practices of Hinduism or the sensual rhythms of African chant. Buddhist chant invokes the clarity, emptiness, and compassion of the Buddha's teachings, its spacious and transparent tones inviting us to join those who have:

"Gone. Gone. Gone beyond. Gone beyond the beyond . . ."
"Ga-tay, ga-tay, para ga-tay, para sam ga-tay; bodhi svaha."

Islamic/Sufi Chant

In the mystical softness of predawn Meknès, Morocco, the haunting, beautiful voices of the *muezzins*—the ones who call the faithful to
prayer—chant to each other from their minarets dotted across this
medieval city, their haunting tones interweaving and mingling, rousing the people from sleep. As dawn approaches, they break into the
adhan—the traditional call to prayer:

"Allah hu akbar. Allah hu akbar. Allah hu akbar. Allah hu akbar.
God is great. God is great. God is great. God is great.
As-shadu an la ilaha illallah . . .
As-shadu anna Muhammadan rasullillah . . .
Come to prayer! Come to prayer! . . ."

The faithful begin gathering in the mosque, stopping first for
wudu—ritual ablutions in the splashing courtyard fountain. To sleepy
eyes, the lamp lights reflecting off the star-patterned blue, green, and
yellow ceramic tiles are dazzling. Some early risers are in *sajda*—
prostration before God. At the sound of the second call to prayer,
the men and women form lines on the carpets of rush matting facing
the holy city of Mecca and perform one of the five sacred duties of
all Muslims—the *Salat*. Raising their hands to their ears, palms forward, they all chant: "Allah hu akbar. God is great." The prayer
leader—the *Imam*, meaning "one who stands in front"—begins to
recite the opening verses of the Muslim holy scripture, the Qur'an:

"Bismillah ir-rahman ir-rahim."
"In the name of Allah, the Merciful, the Compassionate.
Praise be to Allah, the Lord of all Worlds . . ."

Though Imams are not selected for their vocal abilities, the chanting of the Qur'an can be beauty to the ears as well as to the soul. American Sufi poet Daniel Abd al-Hayy Moore spoke to me of hearing a famous Egyptian Qur'an reciter: "It was like listening to a concerto by Vivaldi. The Prophet Muhammad, peace be upon him, said to recite the Qur'an beautifully, and this man's vocal musicality and control was exquisite." The Imam intones additional *ayat*, or verses, for the remaining cycles of the prayer, the faithful silently following behind him. According to Abd al-Hayy, "The glory and beauty of the Qur'an sounds both ancient and fresh, urgent and tranquil." The chant mixes with the cooing of the mourning doves in the eaves and the sounds of the world waking up.

When the Imam is done, some of the men gather to begin chanting in the unison Moroccan style known as *warsh*, collectively and energetically intoning verses from the Qur'an on a single tone, following the natural rhythms of the text, occasionally singing higher or lower notes to begin and end phrases. As the sun appears in the sky, the recitation ends, and the men leave the circle to begin the tasks of the day.

Although Islamic tradition in general frowns upon instrumental music as a sensual distraction from a devout life, there exists a rich tradition of chanting Qur'an and intoning prayers. The word *Islam* means "submission," and the essence of the religion is surrender to the will of God as revealed through Muhammad—the Prophet and Messenger. Muhammad was asked if he had produced a miracle such as Moses parting the Red Sea or Jesus raising the dead. Muhammad answered, "My miracle is the Qur'an." This sacred book is considered by Muslims to be the Word of God, and honored are the *hafiz*—those who can recite the entire Qur'an from memory. Islam rests on its traditional Five Pillars: *Shahadah*—the declaration of faith in the One God and the prophethood of Muhammad; to pray five times a day; *Zakat*—to give charity; to fast from dawn until sunset during the month of *Ramadan;* and to make the *Hajj*—the pilgrimage to Mecca. Although some people associate Islam with the Arab world, actually the majority of Muslims live elsewhere—Indonesia, India, Africa, Asia, eastern Europe, and the United States, where it is the largest religion after Christianity. And throughout the domain of Islam—on people's lips, over the radio, and in the mosques—the words of God are chanted everywhere.

While orthodox Muslims have an uneasy relationship to music, most Sufis, the mystical branch of Islam, embrace it. In the words of Sufi author Al Qushayri, music "is forbidden for the masses, so they may preserve their souls . . . but it is recommended for our companions (the Sufis) so they may enliven their hearts."

Among the twisting lanes and walled gardens of the old Fatih district of Istanbul is the headquarters of the Halveti-Jerrahi Sufi order. On any Thursday evening, upon entering the *meydan,* a large carpeted room lit by several beautiful crystal chandeliers, you would see Sufi initiates called *dervishes*—"those who stand at the doorway"—beginning to gather. Wearing white prayer hats, most are in Western clothes, though many of the older men wear *haydariya*—traditional woolen vests. The women are in the balcony, covered modestly in neck-to-ankle dresses and head scarves.

Taking their places on sheepskin mats laid in concentric semicircles on the floor, the dervishes bow as the *Shaykh* (spiritual leader) enters, dressed in a green-and-white turban and full-length black robe. After the Shaykh intones an invocation to the founder of the lineage, everyone chants in unison *salawats*—prayers for the Prophet:

"Allah huma salli Allah seyydına Muhammad . . ."
"God's blessing on the Prophet, his family and his descendants."

The dervishes now begin their most powerful practice of chant—
zhikr (meaning "remembrance"):

"La ilaha illallah . . . La ilaha illallah."
"There is no God but God."

Slowly at first, intoning on a single pitch, they begin to move their heads, circling to the right, up, and down to the left, a gesture said to "put God in the heart."

Suddenly, the Shaykh slaps the floor loudly, and instantly the dervishes raise the pitch of the *zhikr* and begin to speed up:

"La ilaha illallah . . . La ilaha illallah . . .
La ilaha illallah . . ."

Faster and faster they go, again and again the Shaykh slaps the floor several times to raise the pitch and increase the tempo. "La ilaha illallah . . . La ilaha illallah . . ." One or two voices begin to sing counter-melodies to the drumlike chant of the dervishes. As the *zhikr* continues to intensify over the course of the next half-hour, still kneeling side by side, the bodies of the dervishes begin to rotate in circles. The *zhikr* becomes an intensive breathing practice, as the dervishes sharply intake air in the short rhythmic gaps in the chant. In the words of American Shaykh Robert Ragip Frager, "There is a powerful sense of energy, of joy arising in the heart and in the body. You are inexorably pulled into a different state of consciousness, close to God." Finally at its peak, as the dervishes lean way to the right then to the left, perfectly synchronized like trained dancers, the

Shaykh calls out "Il Allah!" and the *zhikr* comes to an immediate stop. There is an exquisite silence, both inner and outer.

Sufi Murshid Elias Amidon described the essence of *zhikr* to me as "Remembering who we are, remembering God, and bringing the Divine into our consciousness through music." Ragip Frager's Shaykh used to say, "The music of *zhikr* is the sound of leaves falling in the Garden of Eden."

While the more conservative Muslims hope to enter heaven through their good actions when they die, the Sufis want to experience heaven by the mercy of Allah while they live. There are said to be as many as 70,000 veils between ourselves and God that must be removed through practices such as *zhikr,* the famous whirling of the Mevlevi dervishes, and the constant struggle with the *nafs*—the false self. Sufis seek annihilation in God—called *fana*—cleaning away the impurities of ego until, in the words of the famous Sufi Saint ibn Arabi, "there is nothing left but the beauty of God."

Jelaluddin Rumi, the great Sufi poet-saint of the thirteenth century, captures the timeless wisdom and passion of Sufism in a way that continues to speak to our hearts. In fact, he is the most widely published poet in the United States today. Rumi tells us again and again how song brings us closer to God:

> "O musician of my soul,
>   play His song
>   play His song with my every breath."
>   —*Rumi*

Many in the West have been exposed to some aspects of Sufism through "Sufi Dancing," or the Dances of Universal Peace, as they are now called. A master of the Indian Chisti Sufi Order, Hazrat Inayat Khan brought his lineage to the West in the early twentieth

century, espousing the fundamental unity of all faiths. The dances
and accompanying chants—which were created in the late 1960s
based on a combination of traditional Sufi practices and folk dancing,
were an important part of my introduction to the spiritual path.
While Muslim Sufis sometimes look askance at those who take
Sufism out of the Muslim context, it is precisely their ecumenical
approach that makes these practices so accessible to non-Muslim
westerners.

Sufi chant covers a wide range of styles—from the hand-clapping
devotional chants of Pakistani Qawwali music to the ritual drumming music chanted in the Wolof tongue of the Qadirya Sufis of
Senegal; from the all-vocal Moroccan chants of the Zaouias (mystic
brotherhoods) to chants accompanied by instruments including the
ney (reed flute), harmonium, oud, and tambur and drums such as
bandir, daf, dolugh, and *tabla.*

> "My tongue has left all impure words,
> It sings His glory day and night:
> Whether I rise or sit down, I can never forget Him,
> For the rhythm of His music beats in my ears."
>
> —*Kabir*

The enormous courtyard of the Great Mosque in Mecca is filled
with tens of thousands of pilgrims—men, women, and children, from
India and Egypt, from Senegal, Malaysia, and New Jersey—fulfilling
the duty of every Muslim to make the Hajj. Wearing ritual white
garments known as *ihram,* the pulsing throng of worshipers circles
seven times around the cubical stone edifice known as the *Kaaba,*
with the sacred black stone in its corner originally placed there by the
prophet Abraham and his son, Ismail. Holding little booklets of
Arabic prayers, this global family chants together:

"Labbaik, Allahumma labbaik; labbaik, la sharika laka labbaik.
Innal-hamda wanni'mata laka-wal mulk, la sharika lak."
"Here I am, O Allah, here I am.
There is no partner with you. (God is One)
Truly all praise and blessings are Yours . . ."

In all the world of chant, there is nothing like the collective sound of the sea of chanting that fills the marble-paved courtyard of the Great Mosque. Abd al-Hayy Moore described Hajj to me as "The slow roar of an ocean of human longing, the word of God intoned from ten thousand lips," and in the center of all this sound sits the Kaaba "in a shaft of silence from the height of heaven."

It is the dream of all the more than a billion Muslims, who every day of their lives have directed their intoned prayers in the direction of Mecca, to one day add their own voices to this collective chant of submission to God. *Inshallah.* God willing.

Jewish Chant

It is Saturday morning in the largest Jewish city in the world—New York City—and observant Jews are gathered for Sabbath prayer. The floor of the *shule,* or "temple," is filled with men wrapped in the traditional striped white *talit,* or prayer shawls, and wearing small round caps called *yamulkes.* The women pray in the balcony behind a partial screen while the men rock back and forth, chanting in the style of prayer known as *davennen.*

If you were to walk into this scene, you would see and hear apparent chaos—a flood of motion and a babble of tongues. But if you were to relax into the sound, you would experience something like an auditory ocean, ripples of chant rising and falling, then occasional waves passing through the room as voices join together in common prayer.

The pulsing and shifting tides of the service are actually being carefully orchestrated by the *chazan,* or cantor, who signals the beginning of each prayer or section of text by singing out in full voice the first line. Instantly, the seemingly unruly crowd unites in prayer, chanting the modes and melodies that each one learned as a child. Behind the murmured tones, there exists an ancient and annotated system (called *trope)* for chanting the Bible, with particular scales and melodies for each book; and musical modes called *nusah ha-tefillah* for every category of prayer and for different holidays, passed on to observant Jews through oral tradition. For over three thousand years the Jewish people have come together to worship in song.

At particular moments in the service, the highly trained chazan reaches deep into his soul and chants an extended prayer, filled with melody and passion. Says chazan Jack Kessler of Philadelphia, "Chant is the point of contact between the human body and the transcendent. My job is to get out of the way and let something larger come through me, to let the inspiration of the sacred words and the sound transport everyone."

"Man is like a ram's horn;
The only sound he makes is that which is blown through him."
—*The Chassidic Masters*

It is time for the powerful prayers known as the *Amidah,* and everyone stands with their feet together—said to be the very position in which angels stand to sing. The room fills with a potent silence as the worshipers inwardly intone the ancient words of the Amidah, ending with the famous verse:

"May the words of my mouth and the meditations of my heart be acceptable in Thy Presence O Lord."

Now the chazan begins to chant the first of the seven blessings of the Amidah—for the *avot,* or ancestors.

"Baruch atah Adonai, Elohaynu valohay avotaynu
v'eemotaynu . . ."

As he approaches the end, everyone together intones the last line:

"Blessed art Thou, O God, shield of Abraham."

The chazan leads the people deeper and deeper into prayer, chanting blessings for holiness, Divine might, and thanksgiving. The cantor is not performing for the congregation, but chants directly to God, for the prayers all begin "Blessed art *Thou.*" At last, he comes to the climax of the Amidah—Birkat Shalom—the Blessing of Peace:

"Sim Shalom tovah oo-v'rachah, chayn va-chesed
v'rachameem . . ."
"Grant peace, goodness, and blessing, grace, mercy and
compassion . . .
Bless us our Father, all of us as one, with the radiant light
of Your face . . ."

The service will continue for some time, as the Jews fulfill the Third Commandment: "Remember the Sabbath Day and keep it holy."

———

From their humble beginnings as a minor Semitic tribe, the Jews have influenced the development of humankind far out of proportion to their numbers. Their faith rests on a tripod of *creation*—the existence of one supreme being who created the universe; *revelation*— God revealed Himself through the Torah (the first five books of the Old Testament), providing the Jews with a code of how to live and to bring holiness into the world; and *redemption*—God brought the Jews out of Egypt and continues to redeem those who act righteously. There is something about the Jews' tenacious holding to their covenant with God that has helped them to survive for three thousand years despite the loss of their homeland, centuries of persecution, and attempted genocide.

Judaism stresses actions over faith. There are 613 *mitzvot,* or good deeds, that Jews are commanded to follow. In the words of the Talmud, the Jewish commentary on the law, "Better that they (the Jews) abandon Me (God) and continue to observe My laws." Unlike religions that see "reality" as an illusion, Judaism sees God as demanding justice and righteousness in this world. In this ethic, we see the seeds of the long history of Jews as social reformers.

"We are here to act. We are life's way of getting things done . . .
   Better a moment of awakening in this world than eternity
   in the world to come."

—*Pirke Avot; early rabbinic sayings*

There is also a rich garden of mystical tradition within Judaism known as the Kabbalah, and one of its finest flowerings is the movement known as Chassidism. Beginning in eighteenth-century eastern Europe, Chassidic masters taught that the path to God was through joy—*simcha*—and said, "Come, I will show you a new way to the Lord—not with words but with song."

It is now Shabbos afternoon, and shadows are lengthening in the Jewish Quarter of Jerusalem. A group of Chassidim are gathered in their tiny synagogue called a *shteeble*. Wearing their traditional attire—black silken gabardine suits and black brimmed hats—all have beards and *payos,* the long forelocks of hair at each side of the face as commanded by Jewish law. Space is always at a premium in the Old City, and about forty men are packed into the small room sitting around the *rebbe's tisch*—the rabbi's table—sharing a sparse meal of *challah* (bread), herring, and some *schnapps* or brandy.

Led by their rebbe, they begin to chant their *niggun*—Yiddish for "tune." It is said that "Nigguns open a window to the secret places of the soul." They begin to chant, always in unison, for harmony is considered a distracting artifice:

"Hey tzo-mo l'cho nafshi koma l'cho b'sori b'retz tzi-yo v'eoyef b'li mayim."
"My soul thirsts for You, My flesh longs for you.
In a dry and weary land where no water is found . . ."

Cries of longing catch in throats brimming with emotion. The Chassids begin rocking back and forth, repeating the niggun over and over and over.

Now they shift into a niggun without words, for, according to the first Lubavitcher Rebbe, "Melody is the outpouring of the soul. Words interrupt the stream of emotion."

"Dai dai ya-dle-dai dai dai. Dai dai ya-dle-dai dai dai . . ."

As the pace begins to pick up, some of the men begin to pound their fists rhythmically on the table:

"Dai dai ya-dle-dai dai dai. Dai dai ya-dle-dai dai dai . . ."

The Chassidic masters say that "Nigguns express not only what is in the heart, but also what overflows from it." Some of the men are on their feet, their swaying beginning to turn into dance. American Chassidic Rebbe Zalman Schachter-Shalomi explained to me "We are really dancing with the Torah, dancing with the Sabbath bride. [Jews are instructed to welcome the Sabbath as one would honor a new bride.] We are dancing with God." As the chant picks up in speed and intensity, in the words of my friend Jewish Renewal Rabbi Tirzah Firestone, "It's as if we were all wicks of flame, all uplifted, blending into one huge flame rising upwards." The chant of the Chassids fills the streets of the Holy City of Jerusalem with *simcha* — joy.

Walking through the Jewish quarter as the Sabbath ends, the sounds of the Chassid niggun are joined by an extraordinary out- pouring of Jewish soul in all the languages of the *diaspora* (the scatter- ing of Jews from their Biblical homeland). We stroll by a building made from the slightly rosy white stone so characteristic of the Old City and look in the open doorway as a group of Jews from Azerbai- jan conduct the *Havdalah* — meaning separation — the simple ritual that separates Shabbos from the rest of the week. As they light the ceremonial candle, fill the wine cup to overflowing, and bless the small silver container of fragrant spices, the Azerbaijanis intone prayers in Hebrew but chant tunes native to Caucasia in Juid — a language blending ancient Persian, Hebrew, Aramean, and Turkish.

Turning a corner, we come upon a party of Yemenite Jews, cele- brating in their own traditional style. Though assimilation has been considerable since their airlifted exodus from Yemen to Israel in 1950, some of the men still wear kaftanlike robes and the women, tradi- tional head scarves. Like Jews everywhere, they adopted not only the clothes but the musical conventions of the countries in which they lived, so they sing in Arabic, improvising by using *makans* (modes) indistinguishable from their former Yemenite neighbors. They chant accompanied by a drummer playing on an oil can, cleverly circumventing the traditional ban on instruments for Yemenite Jews "in exile."

Continuing down the narrow, winding lanes we see in a courtyard a small gathering of *falasha*—Ethiopian Jews—as black in skin color as their former neighbors with whom they lived in peace for many centuries. Still dressed in their Sabbath finery, some of the men wear white turbanlike head wraps while their spiritual leader—the *Cahen*—sways in his gold-embroidered robe to the beat of the drums. In an unusual high whining style, they call and respond through a chant in Ethiopian Amharic and wish each other *Sanbat Salam*—their version of the Hebrew Sabbath greeting, *Shabbat Shalom*.

As if pulled by a spiritual magnet, we are irresistibly drawn to the heart of the Jewish quarter, the physical center of the Jewish people—the Wailing Wall—the last remnant of the Biblical Jewish Temple. By day, the *kotel*—the wall—and its plaza are crowded with worshipers bobbing and praying, families celebrating Bar Mitzvahs, and tourists with their cameras. Supplicants stuff folded pieces of paper containing their handwritten prayers into the cracks of the ancient wall worn smooth by the caresses and kisses of pilgrims for almost two thousand years. Five times a day, the chanted sounds of the Islamic Call to Prayer drift down from the sacred Dome of the Rock located on a hill just above the Wailing Wall. And around the periphery of the plaza, the omnipresent Israeli soldiers carry their Uzi machine guns against the ever-present threat of terrorist attack.

But now it's midnight, the crowds are gone, and you can feel the palpable sense of Spirit that seems to radiate from the *kotel*. Standing only inches from the wall, a Chassid intones softly by himself in one of those private devotions called *sihoth*—"heart to heart." Reb Zalman speaks of such times "when I wrap myself in the talit really tightly. The chant seems to take on a valence, a color and a memory. I stop being so much Zalman and become just a Jew in prayer. And sometimes, rocking up and down, I reflect on the vastness of the universe, and in that moment I'm nothing but a thought in God's mind."

The Chassid swaying by the Wailing Wall chants a niggun by the great Rebbe Nachman of Bratslav:

"I lift my hands to You in prayer.
Grant me strength to stand alone.
You are the one to whom I belong.
I'll sing my song to You, and give You all that is in my heart."

The chanter, now close to his God, reaches back in time to draw on his 3200-year lineage and reaches out to the souls of Jews all over the world, as he intones the prayer closest to a credo for Jews, the prayer for awakening and for going to sleep, the prayer that the devout Jew hopes to place on his dying lips:

"Sh'ma Yisra'el Adonai Elohaynu Adonai Echad."
"Here O Israel, the Lord our God, the Lord is One."

Shamanic Chanting

Icy winds whip across the expanse of snow-covered tundra, howling over the frozen waters of the Lena River, shaking the frame of the aging *yurt*—a circular portable dwelling. Here, more than three thousand miles north of Moscow, at the edge of the Arctic Circle in the vast reaches of Siberia, an elderly Yakut shaman—called an *ojuna*—begins his healing ritual for a woman who has been sick for more than two full moons. WhooAh. WhooAh. Ayaaa. Ayaaa, he chants in

moaning, elongated tones. The air is pungent with the smell of to-
bacco, and a crackling fire casts dancing yellow lights across the rough
interior of this simple round dwelling. The flat iron pendants on his
shaman's robe glitter in the firelight—the hole through the center of
each an ancient symbol of the ice hole through which he must descend
in order to enter the domain of the Spirits. Once there, the shaman
must fight to recapture this woman's soul from the clutches of the
abaasy, or the devouring Spirits that have caused her illness.

Intoning a ayaaa, ayaaa, he begins to drum and dance along with
the chant, his noisy coat with its copper bells and rattles clanking
along in rhythm. The shaman is now in an ecstatic trance, eyes
closed, his body moving with the punctuated lines of the chant.
Although he is a solitary traveler into the Spirit world, he is assisted
by the powerful *Uluu-Toyon,* head of the Spirits of the "upper
world" and the patron of shamans. He has performed this ritual
hundreds of times and has always found his way back from this heroic
journey, but one must always be careful in transiting worlds. The
shaman's body is attached to a chain vigilantly held by his assistant
and will be pulled home should he "become lost."

Along the sandy shore of Lake Huron nestled in a green wood-
land, a *wabeno,* an Ojibwe shaman, is beginning a healing ritual. The
Ojibwe, called Chippewa, Cree, or Anishinabe depending upon location, were once the largest and most powerful of the Great Lakes
tribes. Like his ancestors, this Native American shaman has gone
alone into the wilderness—a vision quest—where sacred and secret
chants were revealed to him for use in healing. Drums and rattles
keep a steady pulse as he begins to dance and chant himself into the
ecstatic state common to shamanic ritual. Reaching down into the
ceremonial fire, he picks up hot coals with his bare hands. The healer
then rubs his hot hands on his "patient" singing: "Gaa wiin daa-
aangoshkigaazo ahaw enaabiyaan gaainaabid"—"You cannot destroy
one who has dreamed a dream like mine."

The English word *shaman* comes from the Tungusic language of Siberia—*saman*—broadly meaning "mastery over fire," "magical flight," and "communion with Spirit." Shamans are skilled in healing body, mind, and Spirit, and through the use of sound and other techniques, are trained to serve as a conduit between everyday life and the world of Spirit. Called by a variety of names—"medicine woman," "wizard," "sorcerer," "curandero," "witch doctor," "man or woman of power"—shamans are revered in virtually every indigenous culture on every continent. For as long as there have been people in community, there have been such healers—among the seventeen-thousand-year-old cave paintings at Les Trois Frères in France, we see a shaman playing a resonating musical bow.

But shamans are not merely exotic figures from a rapidly disappearing world. Oscar Miro-Quesada, a Peruvian shamanic practitioner initiated in the Andean Paqokuna and Huachuma curandero traditions, is also a trained researcher and psychologist, living many of the externals of a contemporary Western life. According to Oscar, a shaman is "one who embarks on a journey through seen and unseen worlds with the intention to heal and restore harmony among people, social institutions, and nature." Oscar performs the same healing work as shamans throughout history, clad in a T-shirt and shorts, except in times of major ceremonies. Drawing on ancestral medicine ways, Oscar Miro-Quesada travels via chant and visionary trance into a state of communion with the unseen world—*"teqse muyu amaru"*—a living universe of fertile energy that contains all primordial sound. For experienced shamans like Oscar, the trance chanting may be almost whispered, but apprentices and those coming for healing are taught to chant loudly, helping them to break through the restrictive barriers conditioned by our "five sensorial-reality" into transcendent planes of existence.

Gathered around their healing altars, or *mesas*, Oscar and his apprentices chant first to *Pachamama*, Mother Earth and the medicine

Spirit of the south: "Pa-cha-ma-ma . . . Pa-cha-ma-ma . . . Pa-cha-ma-ma . . ." Holding the tones out, Oscar's voice literally ripples with high harmonics, sending powerful sonic waves out into the atmosphere. They chant from three to twenty-one times, depending on the ceremonial nature of the healing, sometimes accompanied by rattles and drums. The group then honors the west, invoking the medicine Spirit of Mama Killa, or Grandmother Moon: "Ma-ma-ki-lla . . ." Continuing the ritual, they intone to "Wiracocha," supreme creator and medicine Spirit of the north; Father Inti—Father Sun and medicine Spirit of the west, and K'uychi, the eternal rainbow, holding the sacred center. Through ancestral chant, the mesa becomes consecrated healing ground and is transformed into the physical embodiment in this world of the energy and powers of the world of Spirit.

Like other mystics we have studied, shamans intuitively understand vibration as the nature of reality. In their healing work, they use their mastery of the powers of sound in a number of ways. First, shamans transport themselves into an altered state of being through sound. Cultural anthropologist Joan Halifax told me "Chant is the shaman's path to the transcendent Spirit world."

"O, he le. As I sing I go through the air to a holy place where *Yusum* (the supreme being) will give me power to do wonderful things.

I am surrounded by little clouds, and as I go through the air I change, becoming Spirit only."

—*Geronimo, Apache chief and Holy Man*

In addition to voice, shamans use drums and rattles—called "the sacred celestial horse," the "shaman's canoe," or the "rainbow bridge"—to alter consciousness. The rhythmic drumming of shamans creates frequencies at four to seven cycles per second—the same as theta waves in the brain that are typical of trance states.

Shamans also use chant to invoke the living reality of the ancestors and Spirits. Similar to the Hindu *bija,* the actual vibrations of shamanic chants call the reality of what they represent into being. When a shaman chants the word for "eagle" in a sacred way, the Spirit of the eagle is invoked. Speaking of his *tarjos,* or medicine songs, Oscar told me that "I am singing to the mesa, awakening my vision of the unseen world, inviting the Spirit medicine to come to life. I use toning to call in and potentiate the amount and quality of Spirit medicine offered from the upper, middle, and lower worlds."

Lastly, shamans use sound to shift the vibrational reality of those who have come for healing. Elena Abila is a Chicana *curandera* (healer) trained in the Aztec tradition, now living in New Mexico. Elena described to me how she uses sound to "break up grief that is held in the body and needs to be released." Without further introduction, Elena emitted a series of intense sounds: "Eehh! Eehh! Eehh! Eehh! Eehh!" The sounds kept increasing in volume with an exquisitely piercing resonance that set my entire body vibrating and caused my skull to feel like it was opening on hinges. Then she sang some of the tones she uses in her practice of *corazon cura corazon*—heart healing heart. Her voice transformed into this melodious essence-of-all-mothers-singing-all-lullabies, softly crooning to me until I felt tears begin to well up.

Though some shaman's songs are traditional and taught to them as part of their apprenticeship, others come from the Spirit world, often gifted to the shaman only after rites of deep purification, fasting, pilgrimage, isolation, illness, even ritual physical dismemberment. Shamans believe that healing chants have a life of their own. While visiting a woman healer in India as part of her research, musicologist Pat Moffit Cook had the following experience:

"In response to my questions the healer told me, 'Well, you just go sit in my hut and then later tell me what you felt.' I sat there with my food bowl for some time, not really knowing what she was asking. Then, it was as if the walls began to sing these unfamiliar tunes over and over. It was quite distinct. When I came out and she asked me what had happened, I began to sing her the tunes that I had 'heard.' It turns out that these were her secret healing chants, the ones that were given to her. The healer turned to me and said, 'You see, they're living. They're alive and you should study this.'"

If you listen to recordings of shamanic chant, you will hear sounds that from a musical perspective seem quite strange. As Joan Halifax says, "The chants are not about beauty; they are about changing consciousness." The chant is medicine, and the shaman has but one concern — its power and efficacy.

As it has throughout human history, shamanism continues to evolve and adapt to new conditions. The Foundation for Shamanic Studies in California offers training in shamanic healing, soul retrieval, and shamanic counseling, and distributes CDs of drumming for shamanic journeys. In the national headquarters of some large businesses, people calling themselves "corporate shamans" go about their work of healing the Spirit of the institution and the hearts and souls of those who work there. Their wide range of healing techniques, drawn from psychology, management science, meditation, and the arts, includes the teaching of mantras and drumming and chanting at work team retreats.

Meanwhile, the old ways continue on. In the dusty outback of Australia, the kin of a deceased gather for a collective shamanic rite of transporting the dead man's shattered Spirit through chant into the "Dreamtime." Their songs will not be reprinted here, for in this ancient society, the chants are considered too sacred to ever be heard by the uninitiated. The Aboriginals' ancestors sang the world into being and created the song-lines — the hidden roads of Spirit that travel across the landscape, emanating from every animal, water hole, rock, and tree, always there to guide our next steps. They have an expression which can perhaps remind us of the healing power of sacred sound: "Without the song-lines," the people say, "we could never find our way home."

Earth and Goddess Chants

Deep in a twisting labyrinth of canyons in the wilderness of southern Utah, Judith and I sit with our group of questers in the ritual site, an almost complete circle of red and white sandstone cliffs, several hundred feet high, which we call "the kiva." The quarter moon is just rising, and the ceremonial fire burns high in the center of our circle, casting our giant shadows on the cliff wall. We begin to chant the Arapaho song of the he-wolf calling to the she-wolf: "Woa woa . . . Woa woa . . . Woa woa . . . Woa yeh . . . Yeh yeh . . . Yeh yeh . . ." The sounds reverberate around the rim of the great stone circle. "Woa . . . . . woa . . . . . woa . . . . . woa . . ." Gazing down on us from the cliff wall is a painted petroglyph of a shaman-figure, half-man, half-bird, left many centuries ago by "the ancient ones," the Anasazi Indians, who mysteriously disappeared. "Listen to the wind, carry me . . ." We chant now in English with drums and rattles, the booming sound ricocheting off the cliffs. "Carry me home to myself."

One by one, our white-masked questers stand. Tomorrow they head out alone into the canyons for three days and nights to seek wisdom and healing in solitude. Tonight, they partake in a ritual of severance, as Judith intones poems each person had previously written as if anticipating their physical death. As the drums continue their hypnotic pulsing, one by one the masked figures begin to dance their farewell to life and those they love—every one of their moves mirrored by a fifty-foot archetypal shadow-figure on the cliff wall behind. We chant again, "Listen to the wind . . ." One by one, our courageous seekers speak their farewells and declare their intent. "Carry me home to myself." The drums are like our collective heart-beat, the chant our common voice. We dance, we feel our feet touch the living earth, even as our Spirits drift heavenward with the smoke from our fire. And the wind, breathing out the mouth of the canyon, carries our song . . . carries us "home to ourselves."

The last decades have seen a resurgence of people in Western cultures seeking to reconnect with the living spirituality of the natural world. Not able to find what they needed in their own traditions, people have sought inspiration, practices, and chants from those paths that emphasize a deeper sense of interconnectedness with all life, an intimate relationship with the seasons and natural cycles, and a rever-ence for the earth as our Mother. Many found such inspiration from Native American traditions, drawing on rituals such as vision quests, talking sticks, sweat lodges, drumming, and chant:

"Wearing my long wing feathers as I fly.
I circle around, I circle around. The boundaries of the Earth."
—*Arapaho Ghost Dance Song*

According to Alaskan wilderness teacher David LaChapelle, "Chanting outside transforms our relationship to natural systems—makes us a part of them. This is not a concept—you feel it! I discover landscapes living inside of me, even while I'm living into the external landscape in a deeper way."

Steven and Meredith Foster, founders of the School of Lost Borders, have been pioneers in reintroducing traditional wilderness rites of passage. While having received training with Native Ameri-can elders, they work to create rituals that fit in a contemporary Western context and draw on their own ethnic roots. Their work centers around the vision fast—a rite of passage for those in life transition: teenagers entering adulthood, marriages or divorces, older people seeking elderhood or cronehood.

Before sending people out on the mountain, Steven and Meredith suggest rituals for use during their four days and four nights alone, without food, such as creating a small ceremonial circle of stone, an all-night vigil to greet the dawn, and chanting:

"We talk to them about using the rattle," says Steven, "about how it can be used for healing and to summon Spirits. We demonstrate how whines and moans, cries and howls may emerge out of the rhythm of the rattle. They see how energy can come right out of the earth up through your body and become a wordless chant or song that resonates different places in the heart, or the belly."

Group chant also plays an important role in their work. When questers prepare to depart the "threshold circle" for the mountain, the group always blesses them with this chant:

"We are one with the infinite sun.
Forever, and ever and ever."

When the groups return and enter the ceremonial sauna, according to Steven, "We chant like crazy—all the songs we have learned over the years, and sometimes the ones people have brought back from their time on the mountain."

"The earth, the air, the water, the fire.
Return, return, return, return."

There is a growing body of nature chants such as those, passed from group to group in keeping with the long oral tradition of sacred songs.

———

These new and evolving spiritual paths tend to be decentralized and nonhierarchical. There are no sacred texts to memorize or centuries-old rules to follow. Well-known ceremonial leader Elizabeth Cogburn said to me, "You won't read it in a book. Read yourself, and everything will follow from that." Steven agreed that he and Meredith never tell people exactly what to do, for they want to empower people to access their own wisdom.

But inevitably, over the course of the wilderness quests, out of the boredom, the inspiration, the suffering, and the breakthroughs, chanting arises. I remember a time I led a group of questers into the Sangre de Cristo Mountains of southern Colorado. We were camped in a high alpine meadow, ringed by a bowl of craggy snow-capped peaks forming a horseshoe around us. On the last night of people's solo time, as darkness set in and the temperature dropped, I heard a man's voice begin to intone. His sounds circled around the peaks and echoed back again, louder and louder until the valley seemed filled with his song and his heart. Then one by one, others began to sing, to cry out their passion, their loneliness, their joy and their pain, each in their own way, the whole valley vibrating with sound and chant.

At the heart of the earth-based traditions is the understanding that the Creator lives in the forms of creation, and that by honoring the elements, the celestial bodies, and all living creatures, we honor the Divine. In the words of Elizabeth Cogburn, "Nature is the Body of God." When we cut ourselves off from the living fabric of life, something in us withers. Indian/metis ceremonial leader Brooke Medicine Eagle told me how early in her training she was asked by one of her teachers, "How long has it been since you sang in honor of the flower? How long has it been since you sang in honor of the great whale? How long has it been since you sang in honor of the trees?' I just sat there and cried, because I couldn't remember ever doing it."

Steven Foster tells this story of a time when he was out on the mountain and spotted a group of deer about a hundred yards away. "Without thinking, I just began chanting to them, making up my own version of William Blake's poem:

> 'Wild deer, wild deer
> Wandering here and there
> Keeps the human soul from care.'

"I must have chanted for about ten minutes, while slowly they came toward me, closer and closer until I could have touched them. My legs were folded under me—perhaps they thought I was a singing rock. It was a feeling of being blessed by the deer. But then I realized that we also bless our environment by chanting. We sit under a willow and derive benefit from its shade and beauty, but when we sing to the tree, the willow also receives back from us, as if we had touched the willow with our heart."

> "The Earth is our Mother, we must take care of Her."
> "Hey yana ho hana hey yan yan."

Many others, especially women, have looked toward another source for their spiritual roots—the ancient and long-suppressed Goddess traditions.

In one of those striking juxtapositions of the modern and ancient worlds, twenty-six women drive their cars up to the great monument of Stonehenge, jutting up out of the green plains of central England. Standing tall and stark against the pink sunrise, these ancient granite monoliths have watched centuries pass, empires rise and crumble. The best known of thousands of stone circles throughout Europe, Stonehenge is said by some to be an ancient burial site, a ceremonial calendar marking the seasons, or a primitive observatory tracking the movements of heavenly bodies. We know that throughout its history it has been held as sacred by countless pilgrims and those desiring to perform ritual.

As the sky begins to change from dark to light and the stars fade into the orange rays of the rising sun, the women—teachers, professionals, artists, and musicians—reclaim a sacred ritual based on pagan traditions. They come to evoke the feminine aspect of the Divine and to honor the Earth as the living embodiment of Her Spirit. Entering in procession from the east, these modern priestesses pass between the stones while quietly chanting:

"Earth Mother, I honor your body.
Earth Mother, I sing to your stones.
Earth Mother, I enter your body.
Earth Mother, I honor your bones."

Standing in a circle—mirroring the shape of the great stones—each woman in turn speaks the name of a goddess or woman of power—"Hecate," "Artemis," "Morgana le Fay," "Mary Magdelene." As each name is intoned, the woman gives her body over to spontaneous movements and dance, invoking the unique qualities of that Spirit. "Rhiannon," one woman chants, moving her arms softly and slowly like the wings of a dove, offering devotion to the goddess of birds and song. "Gaia," sings another, as her hands pay homage to the Earth Mother. All the women then bow down and touch the Earth herself with their lips. Breathing in, they draw deep primal feminine earth energy into their own being; then, on the out breath they send it back into the ground, toning each in their own way.

One of the convenors of this ritual was musician and priestess in the Fellowship of Isis, Kay Gardner. "We experienced our Mother, the earth, as a living being. My feet became like roots being pulled by the magnetic force of the earth all the way to its core. At the same time, I felt drawn heavenwards, like I was the meeting place between earth and sky. You could also sense the invisible presence of those across the centuries who have performed ritual on this very spot. We called out to the Goddess, and when she responds, there is always a feeling of awe."

Closer to home, Kay has met every week for the past five years with a circle of up to sixty women. Calling themselves "Women with Wings," they celebrate the feminine Spirit with chants from all traditions that touch the woman's soul, such as:

> "Ancient Mother, I hear you calling.
> Ancient Mother, I hear your song."

Like many such circles around the world, it is a safe and nurturing place for women to find and express their voices in a world where the voices of women have long been stifled.

> "We're a river of birds in migration,
> A nation of women with wings."

The ceremony at Stonehenge and "Women with Wings" represent part of the global rebirth of a feminine, earth-based spirituality. The history of patriarchal religions is being reexamined to discover the hidden voices of women. Bookstore shelves are stocked with titles on women and spirituality—in words, in prayer, and in chant. In small gatherings, conferences and festivals, circles of women come together to honor the feminine face of the Divine. One of this movement's elders, author Z Budapest, says, "There is no division between body and soul. One is not despised and the other glorified. There is no division of the sexes. Both come from the Mother.

There is no division of the sacred and the profane; all is related in the universe and none stands apart from nature. All is nature."

And so, at a time where the dominant "rational" and mechanistic world view sees "progress" as increasing control over our physical environment, many women and men are choosing instead to reclaim their connection to the sacredness of the natural world, and the intuitive, feeling Spirit of the deep feminine:

> "We all come from the Goddess,
> And to Her we shall return . . ."
> —*chant by Z Budapest*

By now we have visited every continent, "hearing" the sounds of sacred chant and drinking from deep wellsprings of Spirit. I hope this global journey has left you eager to hear some of these chants first-hand. In the resource guide at the back of this book you will find a list of my favorite chant recordings in each of the eight traditions, along with some musical scores. It is also my hope that you are inspired to begin chanting some of these sacred sounds on your own, and so we proceed to the next chapter—"Learning to Chant."

Chapter Five

Learning to Chant

"If you cannot teach me to fly, teach me to sing."
—Sir James Barrie

Deirdre is riding alone in her Toyota sedan, the daily commute home more congested than usual. As the all-too-familiar tension begins to creep into her shoulder muscles, she starts humming an "Alleluia" set to the Pachelbel Canon in D. Deirdre's at first barely audible tones begin to grow louder and more confident, and soon the car is vibrating with song: "Al-le-lu-ia . . . Al-le-lu-ia . . . Al-le-lu-ia." Her concern with the traffic is fading. "Al-le-lu-ia." Muscles begin to let go. "Al-le-lu-ia." A feeling of quiet joy and gratitude slowly wells up in Deirdre's heart. "Al-le-lu-ia."

Matt is sitting down to meditate after a few too many hours making sales calls on the telephone. He closes his eyes and listens to his mind racing: "I wonder how the call went . . . if only I had . . . tomorrow I'll have to . . . I'm so agitated it's hard to sit. . . ." Matt begins toning the primordial Sanskrit syllable, "Ommmmm . . . Ommmmm . . . Ommmmm." The long vibrations of sound begin almost instantly to have a calming effect on his racing mind. "Ommmmm . . ." His breathing slows and, soon, so do his pulse and blood pressure. "Ommmmm . . ." As he continues to intone, it feels like taking a refreshing shower—on the inside. Dangling thoughts, disjointed impressions, and traces of the day all disappear into the sound: "Ommmmm."

Sitting on the crest of the hill behind his home, John awaits the first rays of sun while singing:

> "Oh Great Spirit. Earth, sun, sky and sea.
> You are inside and all around me."

His voice is softly nestled in the precious silence of predawn. Then, as dawn turns the day, John's voice also rises to greet the rebirth of light. Taking their cue, birds begin their morning song, a squirrel joins in chattering, while in the background, wind softly rustles aspen leaves. "You are inside and all around me." In a seemingly ordinary yet magical moment, John senses the sound of his voice, the animal calls, and the wind's song, all alive with Spirit ". . . inside and all around me."

Deirdre, Matt, and John are bringing the power of chant into their everyday lives. This chapter is designed to help you, too, find your own voice and learn to chant. To get the most out of it, I encourage you to try the step-by-step exercises. Talking about chant can be fascinating, listening is sublime, but there is such joy in the singing of it!

Your Own Musical Instrument

For those interested in harnessing the power of chant, you are very fortunate. You do not have to buy an expensive, handcrafted, imported instrument, nor study and practice scales for years with a thickly accented martinet for a teacher. You have within you the most magnificent vehicle for healing your body and mind, opening the heart, communing with others, and sending your prayers soaring to the heavens—your own voice.

This remarkable instrument expresses emotion, unites mind and body, and invokes Spirit better than any other. And what's more, it's free, easy to learn, made of all natural, nontoxic, biodegradable materials, and is easily portable.

Finding Your Voice

As young children, each and every one of us enjoyed the natural musicality of our own voice. We would walk around, making up songs, sending our natural voice out into the world, completely unrestrained. As we grew older, we began having experiences that taught us to be self-conscious and inhibited. Perhaps we were told, "Do you know you can't carry a tune?" Or the teacher in third grade said, "You there, dear, in the second row, would you please mouth the words?" We learned to compare the genuineness of our own voice with some external standard—against which we usually came up short. Even now, many of us only feel comfortable singing when we're alone in the car or the shower, and we're sure no one can hear.

This is a sad state of affairs. Feeling self-conscious or inadequate about our singing voices often mirrors the general feelings many of us carry about who we are and how we are seen by others. For those of you who think you're not singers, I want to let you know—you *can* sing. In fact, there is only one voice in the world that sounds like yours. If we remove the socially determined criteria for what "a good voice" is supposed to sound like, your voice, like that of all God's creatures, has its own distinctive beauty. Through the experience of chanting, where the emphasis is on participation rather than the quality of the performance, many people have reclaimed the joy of fully giving their own voices to song.

Our first daughter, Leila, had the mixed blessing of growing up in a very musical household. Her younger sister Danya inherited my musical gift, and our home was often filled with our professional-sounding duets, replete with subtle dynamic shifts and shimmering harmonies. Even though we often sang together as a family, Leila had always felt a little intimidated, and she acquired the habit of holding back her voice. Last year, however, she returned from a forty-day yoga retreat where, for the first time, away from family dynamics, she had immersed herself in chanting. We were sitting around our large wooden dining-room table, singing our traditional grace before the meal, when suddenly I heard a voice I had never heard before. Looking up, I was amazed to hear this full and robust voice coming out of Leila, who had always sung so softly that she was hard to hear. Leila had, for the first time, discovered the joyful expression of her own voice and was soon leading the rest of us in the new chants she had learned.

No matter who you are or what kind of musical experience you may have, you, too, can benefit from and enjoy chant. Let's begin with an exercise designed to help loosen up your voice and your self-consciousness.

∞ ∞ ∞

Exercise #5–1 Chanting a Favorite Song

Pick a favorite song that you know well and are comfortable with. It can be anything from the national anthem to a song by your favorite musical group. Stand up. In a moment, you're going to sing this song. But really sing it—belt it out! Give yourself fully to the singing and the song. Take a couple of deep breaths, and begin . . .

Now stop and reflect. How was that for you? However it was, we're going to take it one step further—that was only the rehearsal.

Take a moment to imagine the best performance you have ever heard of this song. Hear it in your imagination . . . with all its power and feeling.

You are going to sing your song once again, but this time imagine that your rendition will be at least as beautiful as the version in your memory. And this time, the song will be a performance. You are singing for an imaginary audience, an audience who loves the song, and who loves your voice. Their hearts and passions rise and fall with your every note. So this time, hold nothing back. Give it your all. Sing it again, and let it be the performance of a lifetime!

∞ ∞ ∞

You may be wondering, what does belting out a rock song, Broadway show tune, or aria have to do with chant? Many years ago, each Wednesday night I would drive from Massachusetts in a van full of friends to hear a spiritual teacher named Hilda Charlton speak at the cathedral of Saint John the Divine in Manhattan. One night, she told us something that I have never forgotten. In her old, squeaky voice and somewhat daffy manner, she said, "You know, kids [she always called us kids], God doesn't want your puny little egos. God likes big, healthy ones. So give it what you got!"

Chant is passionate. Even when it gets soft and refined, chants wants our fullness, our power, our heart, our guts. Singing a song we love, with joy and gusto, is perfect preparation for "giving what we got" through chant.

You don't need a lot of vocal technique to chant. Chanting is said to be "the breath made audible," and learning to breathe well is the first step in learning to chant.

∞ ∞ ∞

Exercise #5–2 Breathing

Sit up straight. This allows your lungs to expand more fully.

Place one hand on your lower abdomen.

Feel your belly move as you breathe . . . in and out . . . in and out.

Make sure that your belly is expanding out as you breathe in. You can make sure you're doing this correctly by noticing if your hand is being pushed outward away from your spine.

As you exhale, your belly should contract, your hand settling back toward your spine. Try this a number of times.

Now, breathe again into your abdomen. After your belly completely fills with air, only then allow your chest to fill with air as well. Experience your breath like a wave, filling up your belly then rolling up into your chest. And as you exhale, let the wave begin in your chest, emptying the air from your lungs and then rolling down into your abdomen, until your abdomen is fully contracted and empty of air. Do this several times.

Now try removing your hand, but continue breathing and remembering the feeling of the air pushing your hand out and in.

As you continue with the exercise, gradually deepen your breathing. Without any sense of pushing, slowly increase the volume of air coming into your belly. The deepening of breathing should come from your belly—the chest is more like an afterthought.

Do this for several minutes, deepening and relaxing into your breathing. Feel the waves roll in . . . belly up to the chest . . . and roll out again . . . chest into the belly . . . letting go of effort . . . letting the waves of breath breathe *you.*

Exercise #5–3 Chanting from the Belly

Now, drawing in a full and deep breath as we have just learned, sing the tone, "Aaaaah." As you sing the tone, release the breath slowly, first from the belly, then up through the chest. . . . Breathe in again, and sound out, "Aaaaah."

Imagine that there is a column of air resting on your belly extending up through your lungs to your throat. When you sing, visualize this column of air coming all the way from your belly, supporting the tone coming out your mouth. In other words, sing from your belly!

Breathe into your belly and sing, "Aaaaah."

Again—"Aaaaah." And again—"Aaaaaah."

Singing from the belly gives us more air, the ability to sustain our tone longer, and more control over our voice. We initiate a self-rein-forcing cycle: our deep and full breathing helps us to chant, while the elongated and rhythmic musical phrases of chant entrains our breath, making us one with the music.

∞ ∞ ∞

Our First Chant

Now we're ready to start chanting. We will begin with a mantra that you have already been given and one that holds special power and meaning for you—your name.

Although one might not think of it as such, your name is a word of power. Think of the countless times in your life that other people have uttered the sounds that comprise your name. Hear them now—loved ones, the newly-met, seeking your attention, reading your name in a roll call, calling out your name from another room, shouting your name in anger, tenderly whispering your name in a moment of love.

Our name is intimately linked to our sense of self. Say your name out loud several times. What do you experience as you make the sounds by which you are known? The sound of our name reaches deeply into our psyche, triggering a lifetime of associations.

∞ ∞ ∞

Exercise #5–4 Chanting Your Name

In this exercise you will chant, using only your name as lyrics.

Experiment. Chant your name aloud, using only one note—or make up your own melodies. Chant one note per syllable—"Ro-bert . . . Ro-bert . . . Ro-bert." Or let loose a string of notes for each syllable—"Ro-aw-aw-aw-aw ber-er-er-er-t." Chant random notes or repeat the same phrase over and over.

Vocalize with great power, as if you were sending your unique sound to the far reaches of the universe. To avoid straining your voice, support the tone from your diaphragm and keep your throat relaxed. Now chant as softly as you can, whispering your name into the stillness. Make it fun—be playful, humorous. Then imagine that each intoning of your name is like a bell, calling your deeper self awake, calling your soul into full embodiment.

Give yourself fully to chanting the sounds that make up your name. Continue for at least five minutes.

Exercise #5–5 Toning

Now it's time to enjoy letting our voices play with the ancient practice of toning.

Rather than give you precise instructions, think of yourself as an explorer. Your ship is your voice, and you will use it to journey into strange new worlds. I will give you a basic map and some routes to try.

Take a vowel sound, for example: "Ohhhhh!" Stay with it for a long time—four or five minutes. Experiment. Sing "Ohhhhh" on a single note. See if you can make the tone vibrate in different parts of your body. Play with making subtle changes in the shape of your tongue, jaw, and lips while sustaining the tone. Sweep up and down your vocal range chanting, "Ohhhhh!" Try slow, elongated melodies with your vowel sound.

Now try the same with "Eeeeee." Then with "Ahhhhh." And with any other syllables you choose . . . or invent.

Like a bold explorer, cast yourself into the unknown. Give yourself to the toning, and see where it takes you.

∞ ∞ ∞

How to Chant

I have received formal instruction in a number of traditional forms of chant. Sometimes, the rules are quite precise: "Sit cross-legged, spine erect, and touch the tips of your middle fingers to the tips of your thumbs." Or, "Keep your eyes closed, rolling them back in your head as if gazing at the top of your skull." But in another tradition, instead of sitting you may be instructed to "Raise your arms toward the ceiling, start jumping up and down as you rhythmically chant, 'Hoo . . . Hoo . . . Hoo.'" And while in many forms of chant you close the eyes, in Zen Buddhist chant you are often instructed to "Keep your eyes open and gaze at the wall."

When studying chant with a teacher, it is best to follow instructions explicitly, but for our purposes in introducing you to chant, there are no hard-and-fast rules. My suggestions are offered as guidelines, to be tested against your own experience.

What to Do with Your Body

Most often you will be sitting when chanting. It is best to sit up straight, whether in a chair or the floor, perhaps using a cushion. This allows us to breathe more deeply and keeps our body open and available for the sounds of chant to vibrate fully. Many people prefer to close the eyes while chanting, as it helps cut down on outer distractions and may deepen the quality of immersion and surrender. Others chant with their eyes partly or fully open.

As chanting is meant to be an embodied experience of Spirit, it is often good to let your body move when chanting. As we have seen, from Hindu *kirtan* to Jewish *davennen* to Sufi *zhikr,* movement can be an integral part of chant. Trust your body. Don't hold it rigid in imitation of a stone statue of Buddha. You may choose to stand, or sway, or dance. Allow your body to move naturally . . . as the music moves you.

Intention

As we have also learned, intention is crucial to experiencing the full potential of chant. While it's fine to spontaneously break into chant in the shower or walking to the store, sometimes you may want to make a conscious transition from everyday reality to sacred space and sacred time. Prepare a physical space. Sit before your altar, set out flowers, or light a candle. Before chanting, you may want to dedicate the chanting in thought or out loud—to your own soul's joy, to someone you care about, to serve the common good, or to honor God.

Focus and Surrender

Chant calls us in two sometimes paradoxical directions. Chanting is about surrender, about letting go of the habitual control with which we approach most of life. Chanting invites us to let go so completely that the boundary between chanter and chant, between me as separate ego and life, dissolves. Chanting offers us entree into a world liberated from ordinary time and space, along with the possibility of transcending the boundaries of fear and control by which we separate ourselves from the full experience of life.

Yet chanting is also a discipline. If we let our minds wander, we lose the rhythm and the pattern of the music. Even while we are letting go into the chant, we must also maintain an awareness of where we are, of the unique qualities of this moment and the next. In this way, chanting is a practical metaphor for the spiritual path. In the words of the well-known Islamic saying, we "pray to Allah but tie our camel." We learn to reach to the heavens while keeping our feet planted firmly on the earth.

As you begin to vocalize, really give yourself over to the sounds, the words, and the music. Chant with all your heart and soul. Crawl inside the sound, let the repeating vibrations wash over and through you, and lose yourself into the silence between the tones. But stay present. Practice mindfulness. Stay awake.

A major barrier to enjoying chanting is our judging mind. "How long has it been? How much longer should I chant? I'm not doing this right. It's definitely not working. How come I'm not having paranormal experiences yet? What, no white light?"

In chanting, like any meditation practice, we must keep gently bringing our attention back to our chosen focus. One of the reasons chanting works so well is that our focus—the rhythm, melody, and words of the chant—is so strong and compelling. Sometimes when we chant, we easily settle into a deep place, our attention naturally and effortlessly staying with the chant. Other times our minds are agitated, and we may have to gently pull our attention back again and again to the chant. This is completely normal, though our judging mind may constantly be grading us as if our chanting were a college course: "I give this one a 'B.' Pretty good, but not as powerful as that chant last week."

How Long?

How long should you repeat a particular chant? Our modern electronic media-stimulated attention spans tend to be short. At the Omega Institute for Holistic Studies, where my wife and I have taught for many years, a participant once wrote in response to the question, "What didn't you like about your experience here?" the following comment: "I didn't like the meditations. We just sat there."

Chanting is not a thing. Chanting is an experience that always takes place in the present moment. You don't get somewhere in chanting. There are no chanting credits to accrue, no frequent chanter awards to redeem at thirty thousand repetitions.

Having said this, it's good to chant longer rather than shorter. There is a story about an American spiritual seeker who went to India to find enlightenment. High in the Himalayas, he met an old and revered spiritual teacher and asked him, "Sir, how may I achieve enlightenment?" The guru said to him, "Chant 'Om Shri Ram' one million times and you will surely be enlightened." "Oh, thank you, thank you," cried the seeker, but as he turned away he had second thoughts. "But Master, how will I keep track? How will I know when it's a million times?" "Oh, that's easy," said the guru. "You'll be enlightened."

Try pushing your edges a little. With longer periods of chant, we strengthen our chanting "muscles" and deepen in the experience. There is no upper limit—people sometimes chant for many hours . . . or even all night in special rituals. As with any skill, we get better with practice. Our practice of chanting deepens, we learn more, we are further enriched. Experiment. In the end, the greatest wisdom will come from seeing what works for you.

You will also find that by using the same chants, day after day, and year after year, you deepen your relationship to the chants. Through the power of anchoring, they accrue special meaning for you. Your own chants become a special frequency of sound and energy in your life, a familiar and good friend, a constant source of power and inspiration.

Silence

One last important point about chanting. Finish your chant, however long or short, then sit . . . and keep sitting in the silence. The silence after chanting is as meaningful as the chant itself. In some traditions, the main purpose of chanting is to attune you to the inner sound of the Divine. In the words of the German Christian mystic Meister Eckhart, "Nothing in the universe is so like God as silence."

Sit in the silence and breathe. . . . See if you can feel the vibrations of energy set in movement by the chant reverberating in the space around you and inside your own body. Drink in the subtle presence that often seems to linger in the room.

Some Easy Chants

While in just a few pages we will look at making up our own chants, in order to have a chanting practice, you will probably want a repertoire to work with. To get you started, here are some very simple chants from different spiritual traditions, chosen to make it easy for those of you who do not read music. (For those who do read music, I have included scores to some of my favorite chants in the resource section at the end of the book.)

In chanting these ancient and sacred phrases, we are using sounds that were designed to affect our consciousness, to evoke altered states of being, to heal, and to bring us into greater communion with God, Spirit, or whatever we call that experience of a higher power.

∞ ∞ ∞

Chant #1 Om (Hindu)

Of all the Sanskrit sacred syllables, OM is considered the most powerful. OM is not a symbol—the actual vibration of its sound is considered to be the sound of the creative force in the universe, the sound that contains all other sounds.

> "The power of OM is the Self within you . . .
> The human body is a string of OM.
> All that is—inside us, outside us, is born of OM . . .
> The universal sound is OM."
> —the Hindu saint, Nityananda

OM is properly pronounced AUM, made up of three distinct sounds:

A—like the "a" in "amen"
U—like the "oo" in "cool"
M—a long vibrating "mmmmm" sounded on the lips

Try toning AUM several times. As you do so, think of AUM as one continuous changing vowel sound, your lips ever so slowly changing from one vowel sound to the next. "AAAAOOOOMMMMMMMM." And again—"AAAAOOOOMMMMMMMM." And again.

The "A," the sound that is born on the breath, is said to represent Brahma, the aspect of God as creator. The sustaining middle sound, "U," plays the role of Vishnu, the maintainer. And the last sound, "M," which closes only with the end or death of the breath, stands for Shiva, the aspect of God as destroyer.

AUM is chanted on a single note, held for the full length of the breath. As you breathe, make sure to draw in the air deeply from your belly. In the beginning, chant AUM repeatedly for at least five minutes, then gradually extend the time.

Chant #2 Ga-tay ga-tay (Buddhist)

We encountered this famous chant in our "visit" to the Zen center in the last chapter. Part of the famous "Heart Sutra" (sutras are texts containing the words of the Buddha), it is chanted daily in temples and Buddhist centers throughout the world.

This chant is typically sung very slowly. The entire phrase is sung on one musical pitch, and it is a chant in which much of the power lies in the extended toning of the vowels. The rhythm, which is not exact, is best represented in the example on the following page.

The English translation of these ancient Sanskrit words is:

"Gone. Gone. Gone beyond. Gone beyond the beyond. Hail to the one who awakens."

Sing this chant in a *very* low register, with the tones vibrating deep

Heart Sutra

Ga-tay. Ga-tay. Pa-ra Ga-tay. Pa-ra Sam Ga-tay. Bod-hi. Swa-ha.

$_o$= short $\overset{\frown}{\circ}$= long

in your belly. Hold the very last note as long as you comfortably can, letting the sound drift off into the silence. Sit in the silence for a moment, then repeat the line again . . . and again.

This chant speaks of the journey—the journey to the infinite, the journey to the Self. We must go beyond the familiar world in which we have lived. We must go beyond . . . beyond who we think we are, beyond our conditioning, our beliefs, beyond our patterned thinking and feelings. Beyond what we think is beyond . . . and beyond that. We honor those who have led the way with their courage and their example. And we hail or honor that impulse within us that calls us beyond the beyond.

In this Spirit, let us begin to chant: *Ga-tay ga-tay para sam ga-tay.* . . .

Here is a possible variation:

If you have a Tibetan bell, a gong, or any long-lasting, attractive-sounding bell, you may strike it each time after chanting the last word *swaha*. Sit in silence until the bell tone fades away, then begin the line again.

Chant #3 Alleluia (Christian/Jewish)

The word *Alleluia* derives from Hebrew and literally means "praise (ye) the Lord." Though commonly sung in churches, Alleluia also has roots in the Jewish religion, as we see in the psalms of the Old Testament:

"Sing praises unto Him, all ye people
For the mercy of the Lord is great toward us;
And the truth of the Lord is forever. Halleluiah."

(Psalm 117)

Since this is a chant of praise, you may wish to bring your intention to giving joy and thanks to the Spirit.

The chant "Alleluia" has been attached to many different melodies. While you are free to sing any tune you may already know, here we will introduce you to the simple but famous melody from the Baroque composer Johann Pachelbel's Canon in D. (A canon is a simple, repeating musical figure.)

Alleluia to Pachelbel Canon in D

Al - le - lu - ia, Al - le - lu - ia

If you don't read music or know the melody, try singing along with any recording of the Pachelbel Canon, or with the recorded Alleluia chant listed in the resource section.

When I lead groups in chanting Alleluia, some people almost always spontaneously raise their arms heavenward and begin to sway. Try this, or improvise any other movement. Let your body go! "Alleluia!"

Chant #4 Three Wazifas (Sufi)

One of the traditional Sufi practices is the chanting of *wazifas*—the ninety-nine names of Allah. The names, given by Muhammad, represent qualities such as compassion or truth. Among Sufi initiates, the *shaykh* (teacher) will assign to *mureeds* (disciples) specific *wazifas* to chant. These specific practices help them to embody certain divine attributes according to their need.

We will work with three *wazifas,* drawn from the daily Islamic Call to Prayer, that are considered good and useful for all seekers:

1. Subhan Allah (pronounced Soo-baan Al-lah)
   In this *wazifa,* we meditate on the Divine quality of purity. Often obscured behind veils of personality, we chant to invoke this purity that is our true nature.
2. Alhum dullilah (pronounced al-hum du-lee-lah)
   This means "praise God," very much like "Alleluia." As we chant this phrase, we evoke the qualities of joyous devotion to the Divine.
3. Allah hu akbar (pronounced al-lah hoo ak-bar)
   The literal translation is "God is great," but in esoteric practice it is sometimes considered a meditation on the quality of peace as power.

Chant each *wazifa* in turn. Start with Subhan Allah. Begin chanting the words on one note to any rhythm you choose. "Subhan Allah . . . Subhan Allah . . . Subhan Allah." Remember the importance of intention. As you chant, imagine that the very sounds of "Subhan Allah" are evoking the quality of purity in your being. Drop into an easy rhythm and flow. Chant thirty-three repetitions of the *wazifa:* "Subhan Allah . . . Subhan Allah."

When you feel complete, continue with the second and third *wazifas.* You are free to make up simple melodies for each phrase, although they work well on a single tone. A traditional practice is to repeat each of the three *wazifas* thirty-three times. If you would like to extend the chant, repeat each *wazifa* ninety-nine times.

∞ ∞ ∞

Here is a possible variation for you to try. In many forms of chanting, the vocalist is accompanied by a single held note called a drone—for example, the Indian tamboura and harmonium. While chanting the *wazifas*, you may choose to create a drone by holding down a single note on a synthesizer (you can even wedge a piece of paper between the keys) or by repeatedly playing just one note on a stringed instrument such as a piano or guitar. Continue holding this one tone throughout your chanting.

If you can read a little music and want to learn additional chants, please see the resource section. You will find simple chants from the Christian, Jewish, Buddhist, Native American, Hindu, Sufi, African, and Goddess/Earth traditions. Even if you don't read music, do take a look, as most of the chants can be found on recordings.

Making Your Own Chants

While there is great power in traditional chants, as part of your personal chanting practice you are also free to make up your own. Remember—someone, somewhere made up every one of the chants we sing. You can do it too! In this next exercise, you will invent simple melodies and rhythms to give life and power to words of your choice.

∞ ∞ ∞

Exercise # 5–6 Chanting Text

Begin by finding some words that speak to your heart—perhaps a poem, or prayer, or sacred text. Read the words out loud. What do these words evoke in you? To whom are you speaking as you say each of these lines? Now look at the words again. Imagine you are hearing these words being sung. What does the music sound like? What is the style? The ambiance? The feel of the chanting? The rhythm?

Now imagine yourself chanting these words. What will it feel like? In your mind, hear your voice intoning these lines. What does it sound like? To whom are you chanting? Listen for a moment, and imagine what it would be like to give full and uninhibited voice to the words and feeling of this prayer.

Your chant may have only one musical pitch—or be filled with made-up melodies. Very often in this style of chanting text, one alternates among two or three different notes. There are natural rhythms and pauses in the flow of words. If you give yourself to the words, the message, and the feeling, they will carry you. What's most important is not to think about what you are chanting. Let it happen . . . and see what comes.

Now, take your text—and chant.

∞ ∞ ∞

Where Do Chants Come From?

In the last chapter, I described sending an intrepid band of spiritual questers on a rite of passage deep into the desert canyons of Utah, a mysterious, primeval land of red and yellow sandstone, curving walls, and wind-carved obelisks. After three days and nights of solitude in the wilderness, cloistered in pristine silence, the pilgrims returned to camp as dusk deepened into night. As the temperature dropped, we gathered in tight around the ceremonial fire, our shadows once again thrown up large on the overhanging canyon walls. One by one, people shared their stories. And a few had brought back songs that came to them in their solitude. Some of the songs were an intimate telling of one person's unique journey. Others seemed more like a song that gave voice to all our stories, with a melody that invited us to join in as the song repeated again and again:

> "Spirit of the tree, set my soul free.
> Spirit of the storm, let me be reborn."

Often a song is sung, and it lives for but a moment, fading back into formlessness like a sand castle into the sea. But sometimes, a song seems to catch hold of the heart. A few people remember and sing it with their friends, who share it with others, and so on . . . until a new chant has been birthed . . . as it has been done since time beyond time. From where do chants come? From a moment of inspiration, or cast up from the dark night of the soul, born of a longing now given voice, or rising from a simple moment of discovering Spirit in sound.

∞ ∞ ∞

Exercise # 5–7 Spontaneous Chanting

In this exercise, we simply give voice to what we feel in our heart. Chant is essentially prayer that is sung, so in spontaneous chanting, we just add music to our prayers. This is another leap of faith—in more ways than one. For those of you already comfortable with praying out loud, the leap is to "come ye as little children" and give your prayers wings of song. And for those not accustomed to spoken prayer, let the music carry you past whatever hesitation or discomfort lies between you and giving your soul its rightful voice.

There is little instruction to give, for there is no right way to pray. As I woke up this morning, I felt grateful and this prayer was in my heart and sung softly on my lips. As a warm-up, try chanting these words, with whatever melody or rhythm you feel. Don't think about it—just begin.

Holy Spirit. Thank you for this day. Thank you for the air that I breathe, and the water I drink. Thank you for the sun and the stars, for the beauty all around me. Thank you for the love of my family and friends. May this day be filled with joy and wonder. May your presence be as close as my breath.

Now, try it yourself with your own prayer, close your eyes, and give voice to whatever is in your heart, chanting as you go.

∞ ∞ ∞

Affirmations

More than ten years ago, I was diagnosed with a life-threatening melanoma in the pigmented lining at the back of my left eye. From the very beginning of this crisis, I had a clear and strong inner sense that my survival depended on my attending to something within myself that had been too-long ignored. As part of my healing journey, I had to confront parts of myself that had too long been buried from my sight, and ways in which I had turned away from life. While engaging in a variety of healing modalities—conventional and alternative—for many months, I helped focus my attention and found courage by working repeatedly with the mantra, "I choose life."

Many people use such simple repeated phrases—often called affirmations—to help create a shift in awareness or beliefs, as well as for healing. Affirmations are typically spoken out loud or repeated inwardly like personalized mantras. Some examples of affirmations are:

"I am one with Spirit."

"I release control. I embrace the unknown."

"I am filled with life force and vitality."

"I am at peace in this moment."

In working with affirmations, we are creating within our own mind and heart the openness to receive what we long for. Affirmations are a form of conscious reprogramming in which we seek to counterbalance some of our less-useful beliefs and habits of mind. Faced with the threat of my cancer, I desperately wanted to live. "I choose life!" Yet at the same time I had to confront my own feelings of not wanting to face certain things in life, of *not* fully choosing life. I learned how important it is not to use affirmations as a form of denial, in which we mindlessly keep repeating our phrases as a substitute for dealing honestly with what we feel, or as a way of avoiding responsibility for our difficulties.

Setting affirmations to repeated rhythms or melodies gives them added vitality. I found myself chanting my phrase rhythmically: "I choose life . . . I choose life . . . I choose life . . ."

Walking in the hills behind our home in Boulder, Colorado, I would chant: "I choose life." Taking my morning shower, "I choose life." In the joy of holding and rocking my newborn son, "I choose life." In the face of my terror, sitting in the hospital awaiting results of my latest tests, "I choose life." It became my mantra, sometimes residing in the background of my consciousness, sometimes sung in full voice. The words and tones of this simple chant permeated my mind and heart and filled me with the energy I needed to face my fears and to engage with my own struggle for physical survival and spiritual awakening.

∞ ∞ ∞

Exercise #5–8 Chanting Affirmations

Make up your own inspirational phrase or feel free to work with an affirmation that you have heard or read. Write it down on a piece of paper before proceeding.

Now repeat your phrase aloud over and over again. Play around until you find a rhythm that seems to fit with the words.

Begin chanting the affirmation in its new rhythm. You may or may not want to put a melody to it. Often just the rhythm is sufficient.

As you walk through your day, let the affirmation-mantra-chant come into your consciousness. Chant it out loud, whisper it on your lips, or recite it silently and internally. Let the vibration of the words and rhythm fill your being.

∞ ∞ ∞

The eight exercises in this chapter give you many tools with which to create your own chanting practice. But you may have noticed that our focus has been on learning to chant as a solo activity. There is another world of chant, equally filled with wonder and life — the world of chanting with others in "The Communion of Sound."

Chapter Six

The Communion of Sound

"And the more souls who resonate together
The greater the intensity of their love
and, mirror-like, each soul reflects the other."
—Dante

Judith and I are standing onstage before fifteen hundred people in a Kansas City hotel ballroom. In another time and place we might be called shamans or priest and priestess. However, at this annual gathering of the Institute of Noetic Sciences (IONS), we are simply named "conference weavers." Like others of the priestly guild, it is our role to make sure that the prescribed rituals are performed correctly (introducing the speakers and keeping workshops on schedule), to bring people together in community, and to infuse the entire ceremony with the Sacred.

Even to my spotlight-impaired vision, the presence of different castes and tribes is apparent from the range of faces and ceremonial garb. Scanning the crowd, I can see everyone from young initiates to elders. Some are wearing business suits, many are in T-shirts and jeans, others are in African dashikis or Indian saris. It is the opening evening of the conference, and the gathered faithful are clearly excited to be here, though exhausted from their pilgrimages on airplanes, crowded shuttle buses, and the serpentine lines at the hotel registration desk.

Sometimes we chant leaders have it easy. It is always a delight to guide people who are already sitting in the soft silence of a beautiful shrine or temple that emanates peace and spiritual presence. Tonight, the ballroom resonates with the echoes of yesterday's sales meetings and banquets, the air-conditioning feels like it was set near zero, the unyielding chairs seem designed to promote extra visits to the chiropractor, and the cavernous space has the acoustics of the average supermarket.

Fortunately, we come trained in a certain arcane art that helps us deal with situations just like this one — the art and magic of chant! Stepping up to the microphone, I start fingerpicking my guitar and begin:

"It's in every one of us, to be wise . . ."

There are instant smiles and "ahhhs" of recognition from many, for this chant has been a kind of anthem for those in the field of consciousness.

"Find your heart, open up both your eyes . . ."

More and more voices join in:

"We can all know everything, without ever knowing why . . ."

As people begin to sing out something happens. In the words of one participant, "It was like a wave of energy. I could sense it and feel it." Onstage, I feel it too — a palpable experience of people joining their sounds and their hearts, a sense of some kind of force building.

"It's in every one of us, by and by."

After some minutes of chanting these lines something significant begins to happen. My co-author, Kathy, who attended the conference, describes feeling as though she was "no longer in a group of strangers. Everyone was smiling, and some spontaneously reached out and put their arms around each other's shoulders, swaying with the music. The room didn't feel so cold anymore."

Judith and I rarely plan what to chant in advance, trusting that what is needed will become clear in the moment. As we sit in the silence after the last tones die away, I have the strange notion that although people have physically arrived at the conference, it is as if parts of their psyche are still in transit somewhere. The image of calling people to be present comes to mind, which in turn reminds me of the "Chanting Your Name" exercise from the previous chapter. Within moments, there is a sea of fifteen hundred voices singing, intoning, whispering, crying out, and calling forth their names: "Ma-ry . . . Pe-ter . . . Ste-pha-nie"—fifteen hundred personal mantras swirling, pulsing, and weaving. As one person later described it, "I saw images of my mother and my Aunt Laura and heard their voices, lovingly calling my name, mixing with my own and all the many voices in the room. It was filled with memory, and feeling, and tears, as though our very souls were being called."

Sensing that people are now ready to go deeper, I talk some about chanting, and in particular, the powerful mantra *Om Namaha Shivaya*. We begin intoning the ancient Sanskrit syllables, each one designed to trigger the vibrational reality of God. With each repetition, the voices of the individual singers come into greater resonance, the silence between the notes becomes more pure. With each repetition, we deepen into sound and vibration, as fifteen hundred disparate souls—followers of Christian, Jewish, Muslim, Buddhist, Hindu, pagan, and tribal traditions—find a common experience of Spirit through chant.

Group Energy

When I spoke with participants at the conference about their experience of the chanting, the same words kept reappearing: vibration, waves, and again and again—energy.

From one perspective, it's not surprising to hear the word *energy* used, since as we have learned, chant is a manifestation of sound energy. But what are people really talking about? We use the word every day: "His energy was contagious." "The energy in the meeting seemed off." "There was good energy between them." Walk into any space that is filled with people and the moment you enter the door there is an almost palpable feeling of energy. It's the way people talk, the quality of sound, the pace, the timbre of their voices, the feeling tone . . . and something more. Consider these two scenarios:

Scene I. You push open the swinging glass door into a crowded singles bar and are assaulted by a chaotic din of jumbled conversations, alcohol-amplified voices, nervous laughter, an almost frantic quality of people trying too hard to have fun.

Scene II. You enter the chapel through a thick oak door and step into a dimly lit room holding a similar number of people—this time deep in prayer. A reverential silence permeates the room; people are moving slowly or not at all. What sounds there are drift up and reverberate in the high stone ceilings. The very walls seem to radiate back the devotions of centuries of worshipers.

In stepping through each door, even with our eyes closed, we have a visceral and utterly different experience of the two groups of people. I believe that the best way to look at this phenomenon is through understanding fields of energy. The whole experience of chanting in groups can be understood through changes in these group energy fields.

In physics, fields are, quite simply, invisible nonmaterial forces that affect other entities without direct contact. Gravity is a familiar example. It's not a material object—we cannot see it. Yet if you really doubt the existence of energy fields, please hold onto this book tightly, for without the gravitational field radiating from the Earth, you and the book would quickly float to the ceiling. The easiest way to visualize the nature of a field is to hold a magnet over iron filings. We still don't actually see the field, but the filings cluster and reveal its currents of force.

Every human group—your family, you and your co-workers, a

Magnets moving iron filings into the shape of a field

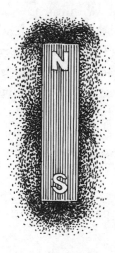

room of people chanting—emanates a similar energy field that radi-ates out into the surrounding environment. Like all fields, group fields are comprised of waves of energy—in this case, coming from all of our individual thoughts, emotions, sounds, and body energy. Like the magnetic field, we can't see it, but we are moved just as surely as the iron filings. When we walk through the door of the singles bar, the entrance to the chapel, or into a room where people are chanting, the group field inexorably affects our breathing, our feeling tone, our own energy. At our Opening the Heart workshops, a number of times I watched nonparticipants enter the seminar room and, much to their surprise, start crying just from the impact of the emotionally charged group field.

The energy field of a group is like a living organism. It changes moment to moment, never exactly the same, swelling and con-tracting, diffusing and sharpening, intensifying and calming.

Group fields are easily influenced by internal and external stimuli. Imagine that you are sitting in a group of people when someone unexpectedly stands up and starts screaming and yelling uncontrolla-bly. Like a herd of animals when it senses danger, there would be an instant and total shift in the group's attention and energy. Group fields are also affected by far less dramatic events: people coming or going, activities beginning or ending, changes in temperature or light. Music, even if it is playing in the background, has this same impact. You may have noticed, for example, how quickly the energy of a party can be altered by changing the music, for example, from an elegant baroque harp concerto to dance music with a driving beat.

The Magic of Group Chant

For those working with groups, chant is like magic because it has such tremendous power to quickly and predictably transform the energy field of an entire group from one state of being to another. When a participant at the IONS conference says, "We went from a bunch of cranky, hungry, tired people—almost like kids past their bedtimes—to this warm and wonderful feeling of connection," she is describing a change in the group field induced by twenty minutes of chanting.

Think of a chant as a template for sound vibrations. The melody, rhythm, vowel tones, harmonics, and meaning of the lyrics represent a pattern of energy. When a group repeatedly intones *Om Namaha Shivaya* or any other chant, the group energy field begins to shift and reassemble around the template of the chant, much like a viscous liquid when poured into a mold. Chant alters group fields by harnessing all the same mechanisms we have previously explored: anchoring, entrainment, breath, sonic effects, and intent.

The transformative power of chanting in groups depends significantly on people being willing to take part. If I started a chant on-stage and no one joined in (one of my recurring fears), not much would happen to the group energy. When we're chanting in a group and the person next to us doesn't sing, we feel their absence—it's as if there is a hole in the group field. If people chant without enthusiasm, the energy field will be decidedly less vibrant and powerful than that of another group singing the same chant wholeheartedly.

Leaders often focus group intent when introducing a chant. At the IONS conference, for example, before beginning *Om Namaha Shivaya* I suggested that people use the chant to honor that place within each of us that is Divine. This kind of instruction helps guide chanters toward a common point of focus, giving shape, coherence, and direction to the group energy field. The group experience would have been very different had I described the mantra as designed to evoke erotic energy and recommended that people visualize their favorite sexual fantasy while chanting.

Once a group actually starts to chant, a number of things begin to happen simultaneously. The "five powers" of chant that we discussed in chapter 3 begin to exert their forces, gradually shifting the consciousness of the participants.

To begin, anchored memories and feelings may be triggered: the smiles on the faces of the audience at IONS when I began the familiar "It's in every one of us," the longing and hope in the eyes of the Jews outside the Moscow synagogue upon hearing the melody of *"Hatikvah,"* the almost two-thousand-year lineage and lifetime of prayer when a Muslim gathering hears the chant, *"Allah hu akbar."* As these associations and emotions are triggered and released in individuals, the tone, texture, and movement of the group energy field begins to change. Not everyone has personal associations with "It's in every one of us," but people are swept along with the wave of recognition and good feeling generated by those who do.

While this associating and triggering is going on, the extended tones and harmonics of chant are transforming the energy field. When groups intone syllables like *Ommmm,* strong repeating vibrations of sound begin to massage their bodies and alter their brain waves, harmonizing individual variations in the field, and establishing a new fundamental frequency for the group—both musically and energetically.

As a group continues to repeat a chant, powerful forces of entrainment come into play. Do you remember from chapter 2 how pendulum clocks side by side begin to swing in the same rhythm? Think of fifteen hundred people, side by side at the beginning of the evening in the IONS ballroom, all vibrating in their own rhythm. We start to chant *Om Namaha Shivaya.* Lips form the "Oh" sound, then a long vibrating "mmmmm" fills the room. Every few seconds, the sound "Sh" from *Shivaya* moves through the sonic field like a windshield washer: "Sh . . . Sh . . . Sh . . ." We begin breathing at the same time in the natural pauses in the text, bringing all the many physiological responses linked to our breath more into alignment with each other. The entrances and exits of consonants lock in together, and the spaces between the phrases start to shimmer in the purity of their silence. Individual voices become more finely blended and tuned, and we start to instinctively follow the subtle musical dynamics in the rising and falling of the melodic lines, hearing and reacting to the subtlest of cues, like a flock of birds simultaneously turning as if joined by invisible threads. Just as Huygens's clock pendulums came to beat in the same rhythm, the fifteen hundred voices and souls are now one harmonious, vibrating field of energy, entrained to the chant.

Chants for All Occasions

Chanting is so extraordinarily useful for groups because each chant represents a different pattern of energy that can potentially transform a group field in a distinct way. Our collection of chants is like a tool box for consciousness, like an artist's palette with its range of colors. Virtually any experience a group is seeking can be invoked or enhanced by chant. Out of this limitless range of experiences, let's look at some of the most common uses for group chanting.

Worship

When we think of chant, we most often think of people coming together to intone in worship. As we have seen, traditions throughout the world draw on the power of chant to invoke the tangible experience of Spirit. It can be as informal as your family chanting the grace before meals, or as prescribed as the chanting of the Heart Sutra in Buddhist temples.

Group chant adds a communal dimension to worship. As my dear friend and Sufi Murshid Elias Amidon describes it, "We're not just sitting on a cushion dealing with our own salvation individually. We mingle our voices, we pray together, we share our deepest selves. This mingling of sound is as intimate as you can get. You're chanting, I'm chanting, and we're melding together. The authenticity of your devotion touches my heart. I allow myself to let go more, and as a result someone else is lifted. It's the great beauty of chanting — we're all in it together, reinforcing, encouraging the sweetness that's beyond words."

Healing

By focusing intent through sound and words, the group field can become a powerful instrument of healing as we have seen in shamanic rituals. Closer to home, contemporary healers in settings from Charismatic churches to therapists' offices to seminars, harness the power of group chant for healing.

At our Opening the Heart workshop, we help participants confront difficult truths and wrestle with their self-destructive patterns, running a gauntlet of emotions from sadness and anger to joy and forgiveness. Late in the evening, the tired seekers cluster in small groups on the rose-colored carpet of the soft-lit pine-ceilinged seminar room. In each group, one person lies down on their back, while others gather in a close circle around them. Upon instruction from the leader about healing touch, hands are gently laid on the person in the center. As the guitar starts to play, the "healers" join in chanting:

"May the love in my heart pass from my hand to yours . . ."

Almost immediately, those receiving the healing touch and the healing currents of chant respond — with tears, some curling up on the floor in the fetal position, others with little sighs of delight — as their bodies and hearts are bathed in love.

"Welcome to this world, dear child,
Welcome to the earth . . ."

The warm vibrations of chant gently ripple around the circles of healing, caressing the bodies and hearts with waves of gentle sound. As one participant describes it, "It was as if I were being sung to by angels."

"Dear friend, dear friend.
Let me tell you how I feel . . ."

The healing chants flow on and on, as those lying on the floor begin to face their own barriers to love: "I tried to turn away, as I always have turned away from love, but the song and the love kept on coming, until thank God, I gave up the fight."

"You have given me your riches . . ."

"There was a lonely place deep inside that I had never let anyone see, and for the first time, I felt seen—and loved."

"I love you so . . ."

Looking at the radiant faces of those chanting and laying on hands, one would surely think they were the ones being healed. Whether a clinic group chants for stress reduction; a sound healer leads a group in toning for health; or a group of friends gathers around a sickbed—healing with chant, like all true healing, is an exchange in which both healed and healer are transformed.

Communion

I called this chapter "The Communion of Sound" because of the extraordinary capacity of chant to bring people together in love. I want to share two very different examples of this power—how chant can be used to enhance sexual union, and a remarkable story of how chant bridged two worlds.

My friend Margot Anand is one of the world's leading authorities on *tantra*, the practice of physical love as a spiritual path. Toning and chant have become important tools in her work, and Margot once told me about her own initiation into the uses of sound in making love.

"I was studying *tantra* with a spiritual master in India who one day instructed me: 'When you make love with your beloved, at the highest moment of excitement, completely relax, lie on each others' chests, and begin to sing the mantra *OM*.' So that evening, when my partner and I were making love, we did just that. I was lying on top, and we opened our mouths and chanted *Ommmm*, letting the sounds resonate in our bellies. It was unbelievable what happened—the boundaries between our two bodies dissolved, we felt as if our two bodies were becoming a cathedral, as if the *OM* were a long echo of our hearts merging in the sound. For the first time I really experienced what all the mystics talk about—where two beings merge and become one. We moved from lust into the dimension of Spirit. The sound became the common vibration in which our two souls met, and truly, we experienced oneness."

Margot now instructs her students to begin lovemaking by toning and chanting together. "It is like tuning two instruments together before the concert, so that when they enter into the lovemaking experience, they are vibrating on the same frequency," she says. *Tantra* is all about energy, and as we have seen, chant powerfully transforms energy fields. Margot encourages us to think of all our love sounds as chanting. "When people start to make these sounds 'ahhh . . . ahhh . . . ahhh . . . ,' they breathe deeply, they relax the throat, and it is the purest expression of their feelings and their ecstatic arousal. Our bodies respond to sound, and sound creates common ground, a common vibration for lovers."

A very different communion experience took place one steamy summer day in Virginia, July 1983. Our forty-person musical performing group, On Wings of Song, was pulling up in front of a most unlikely concert venue: the Pentagon. I watched the faces of the two marine guards who stood at ramrod attention as we arrived, two rainbow-painted school buses announced by a bumper sticker proclaiming "Witches Heal." Our shirtless bus driver, with huge Rastafarian dreadlocks and missing front teeth, opened the doors to unload our cargo of men in white Indian shirts and yoga pants, women in long skirts (one of them breast-feeding), and a motley crew of teenage roadies, twelve kids, and our masseuse. A "closet meditator" in the military had booked us—veterans of peace rallies and healing fairs—to play a lunchtime concert for officers and civilians in the shopping mall inside the Pentagon. I was more than a little nervous, as much of our usual repertoire consisted of antiwar songs and pagan chants. Furthermore, the stakes were high, for NPR's "All Things Considered" had heard about this unlikely event and was taping us for a nationally broadcast news feature to be called "On Wings of Song brings its message of peace to the Pentagon."

From the stage, I looked out at rows of people in uniform and remembered my last performance here—in 1967, when our antiwar chants on the steps outside were welcomed with tear gas. On Wings of Song concerts were about joining together in song and Spirit, but I was face-to-face with an audience that I had always feared. Wrestling with my own discomfort, we began to play.

Our percussionists laid down a solid groove behind the irresistible warmth of our well-tuned choir:

"May the love we're sharing spread its wings,
Fly across the Earth . . ."

I looked out at the audience and saw, somewhat to my surprise, what I always see — smiles, people with their feet tapping, bodies beginning to move with the beat. I saw human faces and real people, not uniforms. I saw people, who perhaps more than anyone, lived every day with the threat of nuclear war and were doing everything they knew how to protect all of us from that danger. My own heart softening, our drummer Marc led us in a prayer for peace. A moment of stillness came over the shopping mall as veterans of peace marches and veterans of foreign wars joined hearts in prayer. And we chanted the chorus to John Lennon's "Imagine":

"You may say I'm a dreamer . . ."

I looked up and saw tears streaming down the face of a ribbon-bedecked officer. I saw a man, who like myself, loved his family and wanted them to grow up in a peaceful world.

"I hope some day you will join us.
And the world will be as one."

And despite the seeming differences between On Wings of Song and our unlikely audience, we were "as one" that day, right there in the shopping mall of the Pentagon.

Fun

We've talked about chanting for the dying, bringing people together, finding God. But have we talked about how much fun it is to chant? When I think about having fun with chant, I remember a raft trip with my "brothers"—David, Marc, and Richard. Calling ourselves the "Gallucci boys," we had set out on a classic "male bonding" experience. In the flatwater between rapids, masculine energy afire, we chanted in full voices a Native American mantra, *"Hey-hey, hey-hey, hey ungawa,"* pounding drumbeats on the sides of the rafts (and occasionally pounding our chests). When the big waves hit, the chant shifted to full-throated roars of the theme song from *Bonanza* as we slammed through the whitewater. Chanting is too much fun to save for "spiritual" occasions. Chant in the hot tub or sauna. Chant with your friends on long road trips. Go with someone to a beautiful place and celebrate with a loaf of bread, a jug of wine, and—chant. Chant mantram. Chant rock and roll. Chant gibberish. But chant.

How to Chant with Others

Chanting with others is one of those things that we learn by doing. Here are five specific practices that can help deepen your experience of chanting in groups.

∞ ∞ ∞

Practice #1: Listen

Listening is the real secret of making music with others. There is a tendency when singing in a group to hear mostly our own voice. In its extreme, we get so lost in our self-expression that we lose contact with the group field, our voice blaring forth like a jazz trumpet in the middle of a Mozart string quartet. Next time, really listen to the voices of your fellow chanters, their sound emanating from all four directions. Listen for the sound that is the meeting place of all the individual sounds—

the moment of blending where the many become one. If there are instruments, let yourself be taken for a ride on the guitar or the drum. Feel the rhythm of the chant pulsing like a living organism. Listen for the music within the music. In the words of T. S. Eliot, "Music heard so deeply that it isn't heard at all."

Practice #2: Let Go

This simple instruction inevitably shows up sooner or later in all spiritual books. "Just let go." Strange how something so easy as not doing anything can seem so hard to do. When teaching new chanters, I always give the instruction, "Give yourself over to the chant so that the chant chants you." Let yourself be molded, as the clay resigns itself to the strong sure hands of the sculptor. As if you were surrendering to the words and caress of your beloved. Just let go.

Practice #3: Give It Your All

And while you're listening and while you're letting go, throw your body, your heart, and your soul into vocalizing. Chant like you are a hungry farmer whose crops may depend on the fervor of your prayers. Chant like you are lost in the wilderness, and the only hope of rescue lies in the reverberating sound of your voice. Chant like you are desperate to share your love, but the only sounds you can utter are *Alhum dullilah* or *Kyrie Eleison*.

Practice #4: Stay Awake

While chanting may take us into trancelike states, this practice is about waking up—waking up out of the trance of everyday life. In chanting, we make important use of the form, the structure of the chant, the text, the melody, and rhythm. While giving ourselves over to the intoxication of ecstatic sound, we always know we are in the chant. While apparently repeating the same chant again and again, we learn to stay mindful of subtle variations, for each moment of music is unique. The repeated form of the chant becomes the ground on which we stand, even as the heat of Sanskrit *kirtan* builds to its fiery peak or the *Alleluia* takes wings and starts to soar. Stay awake.

Practice #5: Just Chant

Don't worry about getting it right—you won't. Actually, you *can't* get it right, because chanting has nothing to do with the notion of getting things right. There's no final exam in this course. The chant leader won't notice if you have an epiphany, nor will he or she see if you blow the next entrance. No one cares. None of this is real. Just keep bringing your attention back to the chant: *Om Namaha Shivaya.* If you are like most people, you occasionally may find yourself looking around and comparing your experience to others while chanting. Perhaps some look Buddha-like in their serenity, while others seem close to orgasms of ecstasy, and you wonder to yourself, "I must not be getting it." What you don't know is that behind many of those impassive or ecstatic-looking expressions run random thoughts like: "How much longer are we going to do this damn chant!" or "It's too high—my voice doesn't sound good in this key." We all get distracted. Bring yourself back to the chant: *Om Namaha Shivaya.* Chanting is a liberating opportunity to leave the world of self-judgment and critical mind behind. *Om Namaha Shivaya.*

Exercise #6–1: The Five Practices

Here is an exercise that gives you a chance to work with each of the five practices we just learned. You will need a CD or tape of chant that is repetitive and easy to sing along with, such as our own *Om Namaha*

Shivaya, Alleluia, or *Shri Ram,* or any of the recordings listed in the resource section. You will do the chant five separate times, once for each of the five practices. These may be done back to back, or spread out over a number of days.

Practice #1: Listen

Turn up the volume or listen with headphones. Chant along softly while placing all your attention on really listening to the voices on the recording. Re-read and follow the instructions for the first practice on page 151. Keep chanting in this way for at least ten minutes.

Practice #2: Let Go

Repeat the recording of the chant. This time, sing a little louder but now follow the instructions in Practice #2 on page 152—and let go. Let go of control, let go of effort, and let go of being concerned with how long to chant. Let go of thinking about the fact that you're chanting.

Practice #3: Give It Your All

This time, really chant from your gut—sing forth with full, strong vocalizations, but take care not to strain your voice. Re-read the instructions in Practice #3 on page 152. Remember to sing from your belly and keep your throat relaxed as we learned in chapter 5. For at least ten minutes, give the world the full passion and fervor of your chanting.

Practice #4: Stay Awake

Play the recording a fourth time. This time, think of it as meditation.

Follow the instructions for Practice #4 on page 152. While you're chanting, be aware that you're chanting. Stay awake. Continue for at least ten minutes.

Practice #5: Just Chant

Just chant with the tape. Don't concern yourself with any of what we just learned. Chant, and let it be what it is. Continue for as long as you like.

∞ ∞ ∞

How to Lead Chant

When I first stepped onto the stage at the IONS conference, I took a few moments to experience the group field before doing anything. All good performers use an intuitive sense to feel their audience. Fine preachers take a moment to tune into their congregation, and workshop leaders, skilled consultants, and social healers use the moment to diagnose a group and what it needs. In leading chant, we work directly with the group energy field, using the pattern of the chant as well as our own energy to help guide the group field into a new constellation. We influence, but we do not control. We serve the group field, but we do not own it. When leading chant, we can hear in our minds and our hearts the opening words to the Saint Francis Prayer of Peace: "Lord, make me an instrument . . ."

Any of you reading this book can learn to lead chant. While I don't want to minimize the refinement of the art of chanting that comes with a lifetime of experience, chant is too wonderful a gift to be limited by the relative scarcity of "professional" chant masters.

Perhaps you are thinking, "Easy for him to say—he's a musician."

Several years ago, I was a participant at a ritual led by a woman whose presence and ease suggested years of leading ceremony. Although her gifts were movement and poetry, several times she intoned a prayer or led the group in chanting. I was struck by the glaring reality that this woman was not at all a "singer"—her sense of pitch was inaccurate, and by conventional standards, her voice was not "pretty." Yet the power that came through her chanting and her ability to bring us together in sound was remarkable.

Even without strong musical skills, one can go a long way solely on desire to serve, the courage to step forward, and the ability to create a rapport with people. Well-known author Joan Boryshenko makes powerful use of chant in her workshops around the world, despite not seeing herself as a "singer." "After a long time of relying on others to provide chanting," she once told me, "I started to lead it myself. I've been astounded how beautiful it sounds. It turns out it's much better if the leader doesn't have a great voice, because it empowers others to bring forth their own voices."

You have probably already led chanting at least a few times. Did you ever lead one or more children in singing "Old MacDonald Had a Farm?" Don Campbell suggests that "Old MacDonald" is actually an American mantra—it even has the elongated vowel tones characteristic of traditional chant: "Eeee-Eye-Eeee-Eye-Ohhhh." It's only a short step from leading "Eeee-Eye-Eeee-Eye-Ohhhh" to "Ahhh-ley-looo-yah." Most of us feel comfortable singing with kids. Isn't it interesting how shy many of us feel when we think of doing the same activity with our peers. Everyone loves to vocalize—kids and grown-up kids—and people always appreciate those who bring the gift of chant. If you're a teacher, chant with your students. If you're a healer, chant with your clients. Chant with your friends. Chant with your family. Like Johnny Appleseed, scatter your path with seeds—seeds of love and joy through chant.

For those of you who still have doubts about this proposition, there is an even easier path. The proliferation of recorded chant in the past few years now makes it possible for you to bring the gift of chant to others without having to stand up and sing. I know massage practitioners who play soft chant to provide healing ambiance during bodywork sessions; seminar leaders who build community and invoke Spirit by having their groups chant along with tapes; chemotherapy nurses who create an atmosphere of safety and comfort by piping chant into treatment rooms; and the director of a small nonprofit who finds that "none of us are musicians, but when we sing along with one of those chanting tapes, it makes for a whole different kind of meeting."

In chapter 3, we witnessed the effects of my leading live chant at the bedside of my dying friend. Here is a story about the director of a hospice program who deeply touched the life of a young physician dying of renal cancer, using only a prerecorded tape of chant.

"Mary was utterly terrified of dying and of leaving her young children. Having rejected organized religion, in desperation she asked me to help her find a way to experience the reality of God. We tried everything—meditations, prayer, reading, discussion—but nothing seemed to help. Two weeks before she died, I brought a tape of *Om Namaha Shivaya* into Mary's hospital room. As it played, we began to chant—we must have kept it up for over an hour. From that day on, the chant played continuously in her hospital room. Mary's husband would join the chant, family members joined the chant, even the nurses joined the chant as it wafted through the hospital hallway. The chant was the *only* thing that brought Mary peace. I said to Mary that she would have a safe passage if she 'went out on the *Om Namaha Shivaya* mantra,' and that there would be helpers to greet her if she would 'take the road of the mantra.' Mary's last words to her husband before she slipped into a coma and died were, 'What road did Susan tell me to take?' And her husband said, 'Take the road of *Om Namaha Shivaya*.' We played *Om Namaha Shivaya* throughout Mary's memorial service."

Whenever two or more of us join together in chant — for worship, healing, or fun — an alchemical process is initiated. Through the power of sound and the shifting of energetic fields, something new is created. The pulsing vibrations of chant become a crucible in which the elements of individual consciousness are refined into the gold of shared Spirit. The boundaries that separate me from you, and us from others, through the magic that is chant, meet and dance and merge in the communion of sound.

Chapter Seven

Chant and Ritual in Daily Life

*"A person should
stir self with poetry,
stand firm in ritual
Complete self in music."*
—Li Yu, ancient Chinese sage

Twelve-year-old Marie has spent the last four days chanting, grinding corn, sleeping alone in a sacred spot, and racing across the desert to the special shouts and songs of her tribe wishing her a long and blessed life. On this occasion of her first menstruation, Marie is being initiated into her Navajo tribe through the ancient *kinaaldá* ceremony. This sacred event relives the myth of the beautiful goddess Changing Woman, how she reached puberty in just four days, and how all the Holy People—those who travel on rainbows, lightning, and sunbeams—came to her *kinaaldá* and sang to her.

The smell of baking cornbread wafts through the hot, dry air, old women sit and talk as they shuck corn, children run through the dusty village laughing and playing, and there is an unmistakable feeling of celebration in the air. Dressed in their best clothes, Marie's people gather into the small log and earth house, or *hogan,* where they bless themselves and honor the four directions with pollen. Ceremonial baskets, pollen pouches, and other symbolic gifts are carefully placed on a special blanket.

And they sing—prescribed chants unchanged for thousands of years, that welcome all Navajo girls into womanhood. Their traditional high-pitched, nasal tones, rich in vibrato, join in singing their gratitude and asking for blessings from Talking God. Everyone joins the "Singer" or male ceremonial practitioner in completing all of the essential ritual songs from the repertoire known as the Blessingway, for the people know that the ceremony's power is inextricably linked to the chants themselves. Later, they take turns choosing to lead optional songs such as "Mountain," "Horse," "Soft Fabrics," "Songs Pertaining to Bad Dreams," and "Songs of the Grasshopper." The people will chant for Marie all night long.

In the morning the Singer closes the ritual with the Navajo chant:

"Blessed is behind, blessed is before,
Blessedness is below, blessedness is above,
Blessedness is extended all around,
as far as the horizons, it is said."

By this point in the sacred ritual of *kinaaldá,* as many as seventy-five different chants have been sung. Now representing Changing Woman herself, Marie will return the guests' blankets and gifts and go alone into the hogan for four more days of quiet and contemplation.

Meanwhile, three hundred miles from where Marie enters the hogan, a thirteen-year-old girl named Rachel enters a Jewish Renewal synagogue in Boulder, Colorado. Official preparation for her rite of passage into womanhood, called a Bat Mitzvah, began one year ago. Rachel worked many, many hours with her tutor, memorizing the ancient Hebrew words of her prescribed readings from the sacred texts. She learned to chant every line in the traditional style called *trope*.

The day before the ceremony, relatives began arriving from Philadelphia, St. Louis, and Los Angeles while Rachel went to the beauty parlor. That afternoon, her mother and two aunts gave her a silk, hand-painted prayer shawl, tying sacred macramé fringes called *tzitzit* in each of the corners while singing "I found great peace under the wings of the *Shechinah*" (the Divine Feminine Presence).

As dusk fell, Rachel and her extended family gathered to celebrate the Sabbath. The smell of fresh-baked *challah* in the air, Rachel and each of her women relatives lit a Sabbath candle as everyone chanted the familiar prayers for lighting the candles, the blessing over the wine, and the *Hamotzee* for breaking bread. Placing their hands on Rachel's head, her father and mother then sang the parental blessing for her protection. After several choruses of *Shalom Aleychem*—the greeting of the Sabbath angels—everyone sat down to eat.

The next morning, Rachel's Bat Mitzvah begins with a circle dance—about a hundred people moving round the drummer and guitar player while chanting Psalm 121: "I lift mine eyes up to the mountains from whence comes my help."

Arranged in a semicircle, the congregation faces the ark, which contains the sacred Torah and is crowned by the eternal light. The room bristles with energy. Rachel stands in front next to the rabbi, and together they lead the congregation in chanting dozens of prayers such as *Elohai neshama*—"O God the soul you have given me is pure," and *Sh'ma Yisra'el*, the essential prayer called the "watchword of the Jewish faith." After a brief silent meditation, Rachel gives a prepared speech, and then steps to the back of the hall.

With great fanfare, the rabbi then calls Rachel forward by chanting her name in Hebrew, while everyone showers the initiate with candy, a blessing of sweetness for her life. The Torah is carefully removed from the ark by the rabbi, then handed down a line of relatives, from oldest to youngest, ending with Rachel, symbolizing the chain of generations. Wrapped in her *talit* (prayer shaw), Rachel chants the traditional blessings and kisses the hand-scribed parchment. Picking up the Yemenite silver filigree pointer in the shape of a hand, Rachel begins to chant. An awesome silence fills the synagogue as Rachel intones the ancient text.

After the closing of the ritual, friends and family spontaneously break into the rousing good luck chant: *Simantov u'mazeltov.* Hands begin clapping and feet begin to move. After a joyous feast and celebration, Rachel goes off with her friends. (Unlike the Navajo, in my Jewish tradition, we get to keep the gifts!)

The Power of Ritual

Like the Navajo and the Jews, every culture has its own rituals to mark important transitions in the life cycles of its people. While the rites of passage for Marie and Rachel are in many ways different, in both hogan and synagogue the community is convened, prayers are said and blessings are asked for, gifts are exchanged, and everyone shares in a feast. The voices of the Navajo ancestors, orally transmitted from generation to generation, and the words of the Jewish prophets preserved in the sacred scrolls of the Torah once again intone their timeless wisdom to a new initiate. Donning their ceremonial garb, both young women, like the heroines of the great myths, emerge from the ritual transformed. And throughout the rituals, breathing life and Spirit into the forms, is chant.

Ritual—from the Latin *ritus,* meaning "to fit together"—helps each of us "fit together" the pieces of our lives—the people, the places, the activities—into a living context of meaning. For every society, ritual has the potential to weave together the separate lives of its people into a collective fabric that binds hearts and souls with threads of belonging and purpose. We human beings have an innate need, a deep hunger, to be a part of something larger than ourselves. And through ritual, we can transcend preoccupation with our daily concerns. In ritual, clock time gives way to the eternal, our individual dramas are played out on the great stage of mythic story, and the known world becomes sacred space—filled with mystery and the living presence of Spirit. Ritual transforms the major life passages of birth and death, puberty and elderhood, the natural cycles of the seasons turning, and darkness giving way to light into vessels for soul.

But as my wife Judith, a gifted ceremonialist, reminds us, "Far from being an escape from the everyday, ritual can also imbue the ordinary activities of our lives with Spirit and meaning." Routine activities—such as eating a family meal, putting the kids to bed, returning home from work, and getting out of bed in the morning—can all become opportunities to remember who we are and why we are here through the help of ritual and chant.

Some of you may be wondering at this point, "This sounds great, but there is very little ritual in my life, and much of what there is feels dry or empty of meaning." You are not alone. Many of us in today's modern world feel this way, and in this chapter we will be looking at how to bring some of the power and magic of ritual back into your life. But first, let's look at the role of chant.

Chant and Ritual

The same elements that give chant its power to heal and transform our consciousness—anchoring, entrainment, breath, sonic effects, and intent—also make chant a potent ally in creating ritual.

Much of ritual's power lies in its evocation of our individual and collective memory. We witness the baptism of a friend's child, and we remember many other baptisms; we think about the ritual bathing of our own child, and we tap into the morphic field of two thousand years of baptisms, all the way back to Jesus washing His disciples in the Sea of Galilee and speaking the words, "Truly, truly, I say to you, unless one is born of water and the Spirit, he cannot enter the kingdom of God" (John 3:5). As we have seen, through the effect of anchoring and triggering, music and chant are almost unparalleled in their power to evoke memory and feeling. We know the songs, and the part of us that usually greets the unknown with vigilance and control relaxes, precisely because we *do* know what will happen next. We relax into the deep familiarity of the music, and a lifetime of memory is touched. When the Navajo chant the Blessingway or the Jew hears the sound of *Sh'ma Yisra'el*—in fact, when any group sings its traditional songs—the full force of its collective heart and soul is released.

The capacity of chant to entrain through repetition is used in ritual to literally bring people together in both body and Spirit. Judith and I always begin rituals with chanting. Standing in front of the room/chapel/amphitheater, we are often greeted by a sense of widely scattered energy among those assembled: people still caught up in the day's events; some animatedly talking to those sitting nearby, while others are lost in their own inner dramas; some eagerly awaiting the ritual, while a grumbly few, having been dragged along, sit with their arms crossed. But as we start to chant, one by one, almost every human being present begins to be touched by the power of song. Attention shifts to the words and music, mouths open and close in unison, everyone breathes together at the end of phrases, slowly coming into a state of psychological resonance, as they become entrained by the chant.

In the *kinaaldá* ceremony, the Navajo chanted while gift giving and foot racing and washing Marie's hair. The Jews at Rachel's Bat Mitzvah lit candles, took down the Torah, and broke bread—all the time accompanied by chant. Interpenetrating the tangible world of their rituals—the speaking and prayers, the dance, the ceremonial artifacts, the performing of symbolic acts—the invisible vibrations of elongated vowel tones and harmonics were at work, massaging bodies and psyche, shifting consciousness into the realm of soul.

Finally, chant unifies and empowers the collective intent that is fundamental to the power of ritual. We witness the bride and groom take their vows, holding them firmly in our love and intent that they may learn to translate those vows into daily action. We can breathe life into that intention by chanting, "Wherever you go I shall go . . . and our love will be the gift of our lives." As we chant, the lovers are literally infused with the power of voices and hearts united in common purpose. Or we gather by the graveside, sharing our intent that the gift of this person and their life be honored and remembered, singing, "Listen, listen, listen to my heart's song. I will never forget you . . ." We tuck our little ones in bed, hoping that in this precious moment of drifting off into the world of sleep and dreams, these vulnerable, beautiful beings will feel safe, protected, and wrapped in our love, singing "I'll cradle you deep, and hold you while angels sing you to sleep."*

Reclaiming Ritual in Our Lives

Many of us in modern society have experienced a profound loss of ritual. The trend toward geographic mobility, isolation, and the breakdown of local community life, along with the secularization of mass society, makes it difficult to share meaningful rituals. Most young people enter adulthood without experiencing true initiation. Graduation ceremonies and retirement parties usually lack the mythic

* Lyrics and music by Cris Williamson

dimension. Children go off to college, childhood homes are disman-
tled, women end their childbearing years, and the moments slip by,
the depth of feeling and importance never fully acknowledged.

In the face of this loss, increasing numbers of people are taking
action to reclaim the living power of ritual. Within institutions where
the potency of ritual has begun to wane, reformers—from Charismatic Catholics to Jewish Renewal—are working to revitalize the
rites of their faith, relying strongly on new forms of music and chant.
There has been a migration from more restrained, cerebral Protestant
services with people sitting in pews singing formal-sounding hymns
toward the charismatic-inspired worship of the Holy Spirit, people
on their feet, hands clapping, moving to the beat of gospel and rock
music, partaking in unrestrained group singing. Bookstores carry titles like *The Art of Ritual* and *New Traditions* for those who want to
make their own rituals. When Judith and I designed our own wedding on the beach at dawn many years ago, few people had ever seen
a marriage that combined traditional Jewish prayers and symbols with
self-created vows, Sufi dancing, African drumming, and chant. Now,
many couples create rituals that reflect the uniqueness of their joining.

Bringing chant and living ritual into major life passages and organized worship is vital, but there still remains the rest of life. Unlike
most indigenous cultures where there is no separation between spiritual worship and daily life, we may spend the bulk of our waking time
in activities that seem disconnected from what we experience in
church or on retreat. Daily ritual and the practice of chant helps us
bring Spirit down from the mountaintops and out of the houses of
worship to infuse our lives with the presence of the Sacred.

The Cycles of Life

In looking at nature, we see how much of life is governed by cycles: seasons turn, light gives way to dark only to return again, water evaporates in the heat of the sun and falls back as rain. In creating ritual, it is useful to understand the cycles of our own life, to see how chant can accentuate the natural rhythms, evoke greater harmony, and give expression to our inner music.

Daily Rituals

Creating regular routines for certain daily rituals helps bring rhythm into lives too often filled with random chaos. We see this principle most fully embodied in the Benedictine monasteries, where year after year, decade after decade, life flows by with each day unfolding in the same rhythm, the same rituals, and the same chants.

While we live in a far faster, more chaotic world than the Benedictine monks, we can still use simple daily rituals to support us in our daily activities and nurture our lives. The trick is finding the time and remembering to do them. This is where the "ritual" comes in. Perhaps we want to chant and meditate for thirty minutes each day. We can try to remember to meditate every day, then go find a place to sit, clean it up, look for something to sit on, and eventually settle in to the exercise. Some days it happens; others not. Or we can have a daily *ritual* of chanting and meditation. We sit each day at a particular time, in a special place that we have prepared—perhaps an altar, alcove, or garden—and sit on our cushion or chair used only for this purpose. The structure of the ritual with its designated hour makes it far more likely that we will actually meditate daily, and by handling all the external details in advance, supports us in taking our inward journey.

Our bodies are biologically encoded to the daily cycles of dark and light. Called circadian rhythms, over one hundred separate bodily functions have been shown to operate in twenty-four-hour cycles, including body temperature, heart rate, hormone levels, and pain sensitivity. Daily rituals are especially beneficial when they are linked to our natural cycles.

Rituals of awakening are one way to infuse your day with the sacred right from the start. As night gives way to dawn and our bodies prepare to wake, our brain waves begin shifting from the delta waves characteristic of deep sleep, to increasing theta waves of the dreamy half-sleep state, finally coming to full wakefulness as our brain begins emitting a higher percentage of beta waves. Rising to meet the day, on the mythic level, we are reenacting the journey from death to rebirth, from darkness to light, as if each day were a new life unto itself. It is said that the first step of a journey sets the direction for everything that follows, and in the words of an old Dutch proverb, "The seeds of the day are best planted in the first hour." What intentions fill our minds and hearts as we set forth on our daily adventure?

All too often, our first thought is something like: "Thursday? Damn! I have to get to work early today, and I haven't made the kids' lunches yet." Within moments, we're off and running, and the tone is set for the day. A more uplifting way to start the day is to join those throughout history who have greeted the return of the sun as an act of magic and grace, and give thanks for this new day. A very simple ritual is to try to catch the first conscious thought of the day and make of it an offering to Spirit, perhaps by toning "OM." You arise out of sleep, your thoughts begin to form, and . . . "Ommmmm." Like a bell calling us to prayer, we use the toning to call us out of half-sleep into true wakefulness. Or you can ritualize the occasion of taking your first step. Rising out of bed, prepare to plant your foot on the earth and softly intone: "May I walk in beauty with every step I take."

Rituals of waking need not be so serious to be meaningful. When our children were younger, we would almost always wake them with a simple song that Judith made up:

> "Good morning, little bird, how are you today?
> Good morning, little bird, we're glad you came to stay
> Good morning, little bird, oh we love you so,
> Good morning little bird, from your head down to your toes."

The line "from your head down to your toes" provided a perfect opportunity to tickle our "little birds" as they squirmed and giggled in delight.

The eating and sharing of food is another rich and important opportunity for ritual. Communal dinners with family or close friends can provide a feeling of a center to lives that are continually spinning off in separate directions of work, school, activities, and relationships. And the concept of a center becomes a vibrational reality if we begin dinner with a chant. For over two decades, our family meals have begun by holding hands and singing: "From thee I receive, to thee I give. Together we share, and from this we live." We've moved from Massachusetts to Colorado, from the mountains to the edge of town, children have grown older, some have left home while others have returned, but when we (and the frequent guests at our informal youth hostel) sit down at the table, the song always evokes the felt experience of our family—"Together we share, and from this we live."

The preparing of food, far from being a tedious chore, can be a contemplative and satisfying experience if, in the words of Saint

Benedict, we make "every pot and pan as sacred as the sacred vessels of the altar." I remember my first yoga retreat in which I was assigned to the kitchen for *seva,* which means "work done in service." We peeled potatoes, broke romaine lettuce, and made several hundred vegetarian appetizers, while our Spirited Sanskrit chanting filled the room, the food, and our hearts with joy as we thanked God, the earth, and all the people who brought this food to our table. Chanting can transform your kitchen into an oasis of Spirit.

There are many other moments in a day that can be sacralized through chant and ritual: washing your body, getting dressed, turning on the ignition of the car, leaving work. Many observant Jews, as a blessing, touch the *mezuzah,* a small amulet containing text from the Torah that is fastened to the frame of the outer door, each time they leave or enter their home. Like many, I work on the telephone long enough that hours go by in a blur of calls. Sitting now by our phone is a plaque made by my daughter Danya with a hand-painted flower and the words from Zen master Thich Nhat Hanh,

"Words can travel thousands of miles.
May my words create mutual understanding and love.
May they be beautiful as gems, as lovely as flowers."

It reminds me to pause for a moment each time before picking up the phone and to be in my heart before speaking. Perhaps instead of installing call waiting, you may want to install the practice of toning or chanting for a moment before making a call.

However the day unfolds, at the end of our daily journey, we prepare to go to sleep. It is an ending, a symbolic death. Many people use rituals of prayers before bed, review the events of the day, or chant, to bring closure and transition into the land of sleep and dreams.

"Thank you for this day, Lord.
Thank you for this day."
—*Chant from the*
Native American Church

∞ ∞ ∞

Exercise #7–1: Daily Rituals

Take some time now to reflect on your daily life, beginning with waking up . . . and continuing all the way until lying down to sleep. Where in this daily cycle might you be served by a simple ritual to bring meaning to an everyday act, help you feel more in touch, bring others into a shared moment of communion, or invoke the sacred? Write down some possibilities on a pad of paper. What might this ritual look like? Let your imagination run free. How might music and chant play a role in each of these rituals? Out of these possibilities, pick one that you would actually like to try. It is better to be successful in regularly performing one daily ritual than sporadically attempting several. What do you need to initiate this ritual? What is the best way to integrate it into your life?

Then, in the mode of life as practice, try it out. Begin today. Enjoy . . . and learn.

∞ ∞ ∞

Weekly Rituals

While our daily cycles are linked to a great natural event—the rising and setting of the sun—the week is a purely human invention. Nevertheless, our societal institutions are so oriented around the seven-day week (and especially the idea of the weekend), that it may feel like a natural occurrence. After all, as the Bible says, God worked hard for six days and took the seventh day off.

The idea of a Sabbath is widely shared, though Muslims, Jews, and Christians celebrate it on different days—Friday, Saturday, and Sunday, respectively. For some, Sabbath is a time to change gears out of the driving pace of the work week, lay back and relax. For others, it is a time to turn our attention inward, to the spiritual. In addition to practicing the rite of a Sabbath day, we can use specific rituals to help us make the transition into its slower rhythm and softer texture. Christians often dress up and attend church together on Sunday morning, welcoming the Lord's Day with song. Jews usher in the Sabbath as if she were a bride—with candles, wine, and chant.

Make your Sabbath the day for chant. Sit down in a beautiful place, let your voice go free, and sound your prayers to God. Put on your favorite recording of chant, turn the volume up, and sing away. Get some friends together and make a circle of song, blending your voices and your hearts. Or go to wherever people chant—your local meditation center, a cathedral, or the Dances of Universal Peace, and immerse yourself in the deep rhythms of sacred sound.

Here are a few other ideas for weekly rituals: a regular date with your beloved, house karma yoga (otherwise known as cleanup), taking stock of the week through talking with others or journal writing, and designated family play time.

∞ ∞ ∞

Exercise #7–2: Weekly Rituals

Repeat the previous exercise by looking at your weekly cycle of life. Are there predictable events in your week that could be made more meaningful through ritual? How might you build in, on a weekly basis, more connection to others, to Spirit, and to life? See what rituals, if any, you may wish to initiate, and determine the role of music and chant in each.

∞ ∞ ∞

Monthly Rituals

Our current calendar system was initially created by Roman Emperor Julius Caesar (who renamed the month of July in his own honor) and based on various mathematical formulas for dividing a solar year into twelve months. However, many other calendar systems are based on the naturally-occurring phenomenon of the moon cycle—the Islamic and Jewish calendars, and those of most indigenous peoples including Native Americans, whose lunar months include Full Snow Moon, Full Hunger Moon, and Green Corn Moon.

While our monthly calendar affects our appointments, the lunar cycle has direct impact on our bodies and psyches. Folk wisdom (backed by some studies) tells us that psychiatric admissions, suicide attempts, and drug overdoses tend to be higher during the full moon, hence the word *lunacy*. The word *menstruation* comes from the Latin word for month, and there is an intimate relationship between women's menstrual cycles and the phases of the moon.

Some women are choosing to resacralize their monthly cycles of menstruation, in many traditions a mysterious and highly ritualized event typically including retreat time in menstrual huts, or *moon lodges,* and ritual baths such as the Jewish *mikvah.* With its strong, tidal pulls, menstruation can become an occasion to withdraw from full-on engagement with life, to create sacred space and time. Here is a verse, sometimes chanted, from a contemporary menstruation ritual:

"I bind myself to my *Self.*
I am Sacred Woman.
I bind myself to all who bleed
who have bled
and who will bleed to Life.
Sacred Woman
I bind myself with Life.
Blessed be."
—*Felicity Artemis Flowers*

In most indigenous cultures, key phases in the lunar cycle were occasions to be marked by ritual. Today, many are reclaiming the rising of the full moon with ceremony. In Native American–inspired rituals, people gather to bless the four directions and drum and chant in the moonlight; neo-pagans and Wiccans gather with candles and incense to chant to the Goddess; and most surprisingly, large groups of young people all over the world, many with no overt spiritual orientation, gather for full-moon drumming circles, ecstatic dancing, and invariably—spontaneous chanting.

The next full moon, try going outside to a place where lights are few and the round lunar goddess—called variously Luna, Hecate, Selene, and Akua'ba—shines forth in her majesty, casting moon shadows over a landscape alive with her mysterious luminescence.

Stand in the field of her light and in a ritual whose origins are lost in time, raise your arms and sing to the moon maiden.

"Mother Moon shine down on me.
I am you and you are me.
And we are part of everything.
We are part of everything."

Or if you are feeling especially moved (and the surrounding neighbors will tolerate the force of your ecstatic expression), take a full breath, and in that traditional form of canine and lupine toning, let out an outrageous hooooowwwwwlllll. . . .

Yearly Rituals

Our bodies are also attuned to the changing of the seasons, the cooling and warming as our Earth makes its journey around the sun, the lengthening and shortening of days, and the shifts in precipitation and wind patterns. Though our inner changes are not as externally visible as the snowshoe rabbit whose fur color transforms from reddish brown to white, or the bear who stores up fat to last during the months of hibernation, we too are affected by the seasons—from the widely spread increase of depression during months of shorter light called seasonal affective disorder (SAD), to allergies, relapses of multiple sclerosis, and increased incidence of PMS.

Most of our holidays are tied to the yearly cycle of seasons. The origins of Christmas and Hanukkah (the Jewish festival of lights) are closely linked to the even more ancient pagan rituals of the winter solstice. Easter and Passover reflect the coming of spring and rebirth, while Thanksgiving and Kwanza are versions of the universal festival of the harvest. Almost all traditional holidays have their special songs, and you can deepen the experience of almost any celebration by including more group singing and chanting.

The one yearly ritual that I would like to specifically mention is the birthday. For most children, birthdays are magical, an exciting time filled with lots of attention and presents. As we enter adulthood, birthdays can be a mixed bag. There may be the expectation that it's supposed to be special, which, of course, may set us up for disappointment. In our youth, feeling immortal, we looked forward with pride to adding another year to our total. But for many of us, as we age we feel more ambivalent, for another year means another year gone. The famous happy birthday chant usually triggers a wide set of mixed emotions and memories.

If you want to bring the sacred more into your life, the day of your birth is an excellent place to begin. Take it as a holy day, as well as a celebration. Make sure to spend some time in solitude. Meditate, reflect on the year just passed, and the year to come. And chant. Among our circle of friends, birthday gatherings are usually an occasion for high play and deep ritual. At one recent celebration, an instructor came to teach us some outrageously sensual salsa dancing. Later, as in many of our birthday "parties," we made a circle on the floor around the birthday "girl," laying on hands, and chanted over and over again:

"We come to honor you, blessed sister.
We come to hold you in our hearts.
We come to thank you for sharing yourself with us.
And to celebrate the gift of your life."

Passages

Weaving through the daily, weekly, lunar, and yearly cycles is the great song cycle of our life—from the opening cries of birth to the innocent melodies of childhood; the brash erratic beat of adolescence giving way to our developing main theme; joining with others in harmony and counterpoint; as we crescendo into fullness, orchestration, and depth; only to slowly fade, until the music of our life, like all songs, reaches its finale. Every one of these great life passages can be marked by ritual and deepened by music and chant.

Priya and Thomas, both in their fifties, recently chose to be married after several years of deepening in love and in trust. Familiar with the power of music from their work as therapists and workshop leaders, they integrated chant throughout their ceremony. In Priya's words, "Thomas and I, our love and our vows, were really the heart of the ceremony, but the music and the chanting was the heartbeat." Like many weddings, the gathering brought together two different families with widely divergent sensibilities, spanned several generations, and bridged multiple social realities. Thomas shared after the wedding, "We knew that if we were going to enter into a sacred ceremony, there would have to be a way of homogenizing the field, bridging all the people that had come carrying all their heartaches and travails, and create sacred space. And that's how we used 'Alleluia' for the opening chant." Priya describes walking down the aisle into the room where people had been chanting: "It was like walking into this womb of goodwill that had been invoked partly by their relationship to us, but also from the experience of chanting together for some minutes before we came in." Each phase of the ritual—the invocation, the sharing of family and friends, the vows, the exchange of rings, and the symbolic binding of hands with a cloth—all had their chants and music. "Chanting for me invokes a feeling of shared emotion, of conscious community," said Thomas. "We could have had a pretty song, but this was really a transmission of Spirit. It was everyone singing together and the repeating over and over that entranced us. It was cyclical, just like the seasons, just like life."

Many years ago, I was a consultant to the Pediatric Oncology Unit of a major urban hospital. In what became a yearly ritual, each December I would lead a memorial service for all the children who had died during the previous year. It was always a bit of a shock to stand in front of this particular crowd of several hundred — parents of the dead children, usually so overwhelmed with feeling that they couldn't look up from their protective cocoons; surviving brothers and sisters, restless and full of life despite their loss; and doctors, nurses, and social workers, trying to look professional and as much in need of healing as anyone, for their losses are never-ending.

Finding a common container for Spirit in a diverse group is always a sensitive matter — clearly not an evening for *Om Namaha Shivaya*. I invited people to sing:

"Listen, listen, listen to my heart's song.
I will never forget you, I will never forsake you."

The sweetness of the music and the all-too-relevant lyrics triggered an instant flood of emotion filling the room. As voices softly joined in song, the sense of community, though wounded and tentative, began to grow. At my suggestion, people then closed their eyes and imagined the face of their dead child/brother/sister, as if their presence, their Spirit, were here in the room. As I chanted softly, in the privacy of their own hearts people shared words, feelings, and tears in this moment of remembrance. When eyes opened, we watched slides of the children — younger pictures when they were still healthy, or children bald from chemotherapy, most of them smiling, some very sick-looking and hooked up to IVs. Faces appeared on the screen, then dissolved into nothingness, while with voices cracking, and some breaking down into sobs of grief, we chanted:

"May the long time sun shine upon you.
All love surround you.
And the pure light within you.
Guide your way home."

The surviving children then stepped forward, each lighting a long thin taper in honor of their dead brother or sister, while we sang:

"Go in beauty, peace be with you.
Till we meet again in the light."

Finally, after a moment of silent, shared grief, people reached out and held hands, reestablishing the bond with the living, finding connection and some comfort in joining with those few who really do know what it's like to lose a child.

"From thee I receive, to thee I give.
Together we share, and from this we live."

Of course, rituals can be far less formal, while still serving to mark an important occasion. Upon leaving a four-year stint as president of a consulting company, Judith and my friends guided me through a whimsical but truly liberating ceremony. After dressing me in a business suit and tie, I was given a pair of scissors. To ecstatic drumming and rhythmic shouts of encouragement, with a wild gleam in my eyes, I shredded the tie—the symbolic noose that separates mind from heart. I then ceremonially burned the scraps in a spaghetti pot— which immediately began belching puffs of toxic smoke into the living room. Fortunately for our lungs, I was then led outside—blindfolded—and taken on a walk, my friends surrounding me with song. Behind our house in Boulder is a reservoir where swimming is strictly forbidden. In an act of liberation from the confines of convention (and release from my one and only "normal" job in this lifetime), I was walked into the reservoir—suit and all. We howled, we whooped, I tore off my suit—an outrageously zesty rite of passage.

In the following exercise you will have the opportunity to look at using the power of chant and ritual to honor your own life transitions.

∞ ∞ ∞

Exercise #7–3: Rite of Passage

Reflect on the next upcoming major life passage for yourself or a loved one. How might you use ritual to give this transition its full depth and meaning? What would your ritual look like? How could music and chant play their special role in giving life to the ritual?

∞ ∞ ∞

The Art of Ritual

It is important to avoid performing ritual solely for ritual's sake. There must be a sensitive interplay between our "enlightened" ideas about bringing ritual into our lives and "reality." We need to experiment with rituals, learn about what works—and learn even more from what doesn't. We ritual-makers must continually do midcourse corrections, refine rituals, and let them evolve over time as life unfolds. If last year's ritual no longer seemed enlivened, we may need to release old forms and let new ones evolve—or risk sitting through the same kind of empty rituals against which many of us rebelled.

By now, you may be getting a distorted picture of family life in the Gass household from all the descriptions of waking and rising with song and holding hands before meals. Though our family life has been rich and loving, like all families we have our share of conflict and breakdowns. Our least successful ritual was "family time." The vision was to take every Sunday dinner and evening as a designated time to be together, have fun, and have "meaningful" experiences. Instead it was a weekly disaster. Every Sunday we all struggled with dropping what we were doing to start "family time," we disagreed about what to eat, and fought over what to do. We should have named it "shadow time," for it unfailingly brought out the beast in everyone. Meanwhile, other times during the week we naturally fell into happy moments of shared life and activity—rarely planned. After about six months, without discussion, "family time" disappeared into oblivion like a bad sitcom quietly pulled off the air.

Sixteen Ways to Make Your Life Sing with Chant

Planned rituals are great, but by giving free and bold rein to our imagination, chant can enliven our life in unexpected ways. Here are some ideas that others have tried:

1. Make your car a moving sanctuary. Put a sign on the dashboard that says "Breathe," lay in a supply of sing-along-style chanting tapes, roll your windows down (or up), and cruise.

2. When you have one of those oral fixations that is about to result in your bingeing on foods you really shouldn't eat, try substituting the oral delights of chanting.

3. Light a candle in the bedroom, sit your beloved on the bed, and serenade him or her with a love song.

4. While walking or hiking, find or make up a mantra with a good rhythm and chant it to the beat of your steps. One of my favorites is: "Your sacred ground I walk upon, with every step I take."

5. Use the good resonance and relative privacy of the shower as a great opportunity for ecstatic chanting. Let loose your voice — all the way!

6. Play recordings of chant in the background as mood enhancers. When you're pushing too hard and need to relax, play a slow mantric chant. When you're sluggish and need to pick up your energy, put on an ecstatic chant.

7. Over the next few months, take a tour of all the forms of chant that exist in your area. Visit churches, temples, ashrams, monasteries — you might even stop by cheerleading practice for a local sports team.

8. If you have a wake-up function on your CD or cassette player (and you have a clue how it works), program it to bring you gently out of sleep with the sounds of chant.

9. Visit a friend's baby and give your friend an hour off. Hold the baby, and chant to it. Babies love it, you'll love it, and they never criticize your singing voice.

10. Use chant to transform your moods. When you're feeling hurt or angry, instead of falling into a psychic hole or running through obsessive thoughts hour after hour, throw yourself into spontaneous chanting — loud vocalizations of nonsense syllables and noises, rhythmic shouts, exaggerated displays of affect — pour all of your emotional energy into the chant. And see what happens.

11. Find a place with great reverberation — a church, a room with very high ceilings, stairwells of public buildings, under-

ground garages, squash and racquetball courts—and take advantage of the extraordinary resonance to play with long vowel tones.

12. Locate someone who leads chants in your area. Host a gathering for your friends called "Some En-chanted Evening," and with the help of the chant leader, introduce your social circle to the joys of chanting.

13. In our busy lives, we seem to spend an inordinate amount of time waiting—at traffic lights, "on hold" on the telephone, in doctors' offices. Never wait again!!! Transform these frustrating experiences, by using each of them as perfect opportunities for your chanting practice. (In public, you may prefer to chant inwardly and silently.)

14. Chant to your plants—in the house and in the garden. Imagine that in some way they're also singing with you. Blend your vocal sound with the imaginary sounds of the plants. You may or may not grow gargantuan plants, but it's great fun.

15. Visit a friend who's sick or disabled, at home or in the hospital. Sit by their bed, and with or without the help of a recording, bring them the gift of chant.

16. Spread the good energy. Play chant in the background while you record a new greeting for your telephone answering machine.

These suggestions, while offered in a lighthearted manner, are exactly the kind of rituals and practices that bring Spirit and joy into everyday life. Use them. Change them. Make up your own. May your life be filled with the ritual of chant—in all its many forms.

Chapter Eight

Discovering Spirit in Sound

"Those who know Him cry with one voice:
He is the singer, He the song, and He the music.
He speaks through every tune. He is manifest in every melody."
                                                        —Nazir, Sufi poet

We have seen how peoples of all faiths come together in the communion of chant to worship God, Goddess, Spirit, Lord, Allah, Brahma, Wakan Tanka, Hecate, and the Orishas. We have explored how the triggering of associations, the power of entrainment, breath, sonic effects, and the intent of the chanters combine to give chant its awesome power to transform our consciousness.

Chant is a tool that can be used to inspire souls to awaken or incite mobs to hate. To be wise in using it, we must be clear in our purpose. In the first years of my marriage, having little idea how to deal with conflict, I would sometimes flee from an unpleasant exchange with Judith, storm into the next room and begin chanting OM very loudly—just to make sure she knew I was doing something "spiritual." Needless to say, this particular expression of the universal sound did little to create peace in my marriage. Over time, I discovered that it is much better to chant together to build a field of cooperation and love in your home. Rather than an escape from life, chanting is a remarkable tool that we can use to infuse our lives with Spirit. According to the great spiritual activist Mahatma Gandhi, "The mantra becomes one's staff of life and carries on through every ordeal. Each repetition has a new meaning, each repetition carries you nearer and nearer to God." When he was shot by a Hindu extremist shortly after achieving his goal of independence for India, Gandhi simply uttered his mantra—*Ram*—the name of God, and died.

In order for chant to serve our spiritual awakening, we cultivate chanting as a spiritual practice.

The Practice of Chanting

The concept of "practice" is helpful in our spiritual work, for it lets us know that we are all learners. When I first set forth on the spiritual path, I read many books that talked about enlightenment. Unfortunately, my only models for learning came from years of competitive, achievement-oriented academic training—I imagined enlightenment to be like a super-Ph.D. I figured it would take me about five years, as I had always been a precocious student. That was thirty years ago. I guess I must be a slow learner. My days still fluctuate between moments of remembering, then forgetting, and once again remembering who I am. Sometimes I'm awake; other times I'm just going through the motions.

It turns out that the spiritual path isn't about attaining something or getting somewhere. Our preoccupation with "How am I doing?" or "Am I there yet?" is just more stuff, more background noise that drowns out the music of soul. A spiritual practice is a lifelong commitment to a journey of becoming—a journey with no end.

In practicing a musical instrument, we play our scales, stumble over the difficult passages, and go over them again and again until we have mastery. There are no "mistakes" in practice, because the working and reworking of the places where we stumble is precisely what helps us develop our skills. There are no shortcuts, no quick fixes. We are lifelong learners—even the greatest musicians practice many hours a day.

It is the same in the practice of chanting. We do not wait for inspiration to strike—we chant because it's our practice. Rabbi Zalman Schachter-Shalomi told me that while some days the impulse to *daven* comes naturally, other days "I'm just doing it because it has to be done—otherwise I would get out of touch." We commit to the form of the practice, which helps sustain us through changing moods and erratic energy. Michael Harrison, an accomplished musician and a leader of Sufi chant, talks about the importance of practicing every day in order to "build momentum." He himself does vocal meditation up to three hours each morning.

Practicing the piano, some days our fingers seem thick and clumsy as we trip over our scales; other days our fingers seem to dance sprightly on the keyboard. The practice of chant is also like this. Joyce Wells, a chant leader for Siddha yoga, tells us, "Sometimes in chanting, I'll find myself after five minutes deep in meditation, and I didn't even know it. Other times, I can't even get into it." We learn to let go of evaluating our experience on any given day—we soar, we crash, we're ecstatic, we're bored, we're focused, we're asleep—it's all practice.

As a spiritual practice, chant has some advantages. It is free, safe, and can be done anywhere, anytime. According to Joyce Wells, "Chanting is so simple to do—anytime, anywhere. It's the easiest path to God." Swami Akandananda, also of Siddha yoga, agrees:

"The beauty of chanting is that it is very easy to reach a state of absorption. People who may have difficulty meditating because their minds are busy and are not comfortable sitting, when they hear beautiful hymns to their own divine Self, when they feel the rhythm and the clapping, when they are able to focus their ears, focus their heart, and focus their body—when all of these come together, people have deep experiences in chanting that they don't have until after many years in meditation."

One of the great challenges many of us face on the spiritual path is how to deal with our judging, analytic faculties. Our rational mind is a great tool, the product of tens of thousands of years of evolution. It has only one major design flaw—the lack of an "off" switch. Our poor intellect struggles with the mystical experience because the reality of Spirit transcends words and concepts. As author and teacher Ram Dass likes to say, "The best the mind can do is say, 'It went thatta way!'" Chanting completely bypasses the intellect, short-circuiting our concepts, our questions and doubts about Spirit. Sufi Murshid Elias Amidon once said to me, "What's great about chanting is that it cuts free from the volumes and libraries full of mysticism and words trying to say the ineffable. It's the real thing."

In chanting, there's no intermediary—everyone has equal opportunity for a personal and direct experience of Spirit. As we have seen, the great mystical traditions of the world share a resonant core of Spirit. Chant evokes the living, vibrational reality of these core truths: devotion, stillness, praise, and oneness.

Devotion

Dinabandu, a former resident of the Kripalu Yoga Center in Lenox, Massachusetts, tells the following story:

"As the harmonium began the familiar melody to *Shivaya natraja*,

I looked up at the portrait of Bapaji over the altar. In his face I saw reflected the embodiment of total devotion to God. More than anything, I want to give that love. As the chant began to pick up speed, I rose to my feet and began to dance.

"Shi-va-ya na-tra-ja, Shi-va-ya na-tra-ja, Shi-va-ya na-tra-ja. My body was vibrating to the dum-dum-dum of the bass drum, the rhythm of the *mridingam* rippling on my skin, and riding over everything the ching-ching-ching-ching of the finger cymbals. I jumped as high as I could, landing in time with the boom of the big drum. Higher and higher I flew—it felt like my head would surely touch the ceiling. Shi-va-ya na-tra-ja, Shi-va-ya Shi-va-ya! I was surrounded and uplifted by the chanting voices of my brothers and sisters, and I experienced their love, and they mine. We were all vibrating with our love for God.

"There was a mysterious but familiar sense of timelessness, like I had chanted these words in ten thousand lifetimes, in ten thousand rooms and fields and torchlit caves. In the ancient stories, Shiva dances on a cosmic drum, and with each eternal beat of the drum the universe is created, then destroyed with the next. I felt that. Dum! And the world flickered out of existence for a moment. Dum! And it reappeared. I experienced how ephemeral this life is, but that God's love is eternal.

"My eyes were closed, and energy streamed up from my heart and out the top of my head. I gave myself, all of me, without reservation, over to my love for God."

In this story, we can feel the power of devotional chant. We sing love songs to God from the depths of our heart. It's all about the intensity of the longing. Rather than trying to transcend desire, or cultivate detachment as in the Buddhist tradition, we give ourselves completely to desire. But all our desires—for sex, for power, for fame, for Häagen-Dazs Chocolate Chocolate-Chip ice cream—are funneled into one desire: for God. There is a hunger, an urgency in devotional chanting. We completely abandon ourselves to the chant. You're distracted? Chant more passionately. You're tired? Chant as if your life depended on it.

> "You've been walking the ocean's edge,
> holding up your robes to keep them dry.
> You must dive naked under, and deeper,
> a thousand times deeper . . ."
>
> —*Rumi*

Like the rising heat of passion in sexual union, the candle flame of our longing bursts into a conflagration, fueled by the intensity of our yearning. We chant and chant, until all our other desires are consumed in the one desire. We chant and chant until there is only the yearning:

> "This is how I would die into the love I have for you:
> as pieces of cloud dissolve in sunlight."
>
> —*Rumi*

In devotional practice, we are the lover and God is the Beloved. This consuming love for God may have an erotic quality. Mirabai, a Hindu saint of the thirteenth century, gave up her life of wealth and wandered in search of the God Krishna. Composing over five thousand songs of Divine love, she wandered barefoot from village to village singing and dancing. Imagine the ecstatic Mirabai chanting these phrases, her voice filled with yearning for her Beloved:

> "Come to my bedroom.
> I've scattered fresh buds on the couch,
> Perfumed my body."

God is there to fully meet Mirabai's love, as the Divine always does when the seeker's longing is pure:

"My friend, the stain of the Great Dancer has penetrated my
my body.
I drank the cup of music and I am hopelessly drunk."

And having tasted the nectar of God's love, Mirabai is His forever:

"Like a bee trapped for life in the closing of the sweet flower,
Mira has offered herself to her Lord."

In devotional practice, what is important is the yearning, the dance of lover and beloved. As Ram Dass describes it, "Your delight is in getting closer and closer . . . so devotion becomes like a long, extended foreplay: not getting lost in the orgasmic moment of merging, staying just barely separate, but separate."

Sufi Elias Amidon agrees about the importance of the yearning. "My teacher always said that it's not so much that we adore God's presence, as we adore His absence. By allowing God to be absent, we allow the mysterious. The longing and yearning create a space for the unknown, and in that unknown lies the possibility of real experience."

Devotional chanting is also a part of the Christian mystical tradition. In the well-known book *Way of the Pilgrim* from the Eastern Orthodox Church, the author describes his experience wandering through the nineteenth-century Russian countryside while continually intoning the prayer: "Lord Jesus Christ have mercy on me." Chanting day after day, month after month, he finds that "the Prayer by its own action passed from my lips to my heart." The pilgrim chants as he walks, chants as he eats, chants as he lies down to sleep, and as he rises. "The Prayer brought sweetness into my heart and made me unaware of everything else."

We find in contemporary Christian gospel music the same outpouring of love for the Divine that we hear in Indian *kirtan*. I once had the good fortune to accompany on piano the Heavenly Echoes, a black gospel group comprised of two big families—parents, children, uncles, and aunts. Far more than a performance, their music is an evocation of love for God.

"I love Him . . . I love Him . . . because He first loved me.
And purchased my soul on Calvary."

The leader of the Heavenly Echoes, Madame Andrews, is a vivacious, open-hearted woman who answers her phone "God bless you," and really means it when she calls you "Dear." She describes their music, "It's really from my heart. I can see Jesus' arms reaching out to me—I can actually *feel* His arms around me. His love is not just words—it's real. I can see Him on the cross, and feel the spiritual connection from Him to me. The presence of God is within me when I sing."

As in other forms of chant, the Heavenly Echoes repeat lines again and again so that everyone sings along:

"That's why I love Him . . . That's why I love Him.
He will deliver me."

"There is a flow when we really sing. Some call it energy—we call it the Spirit of God. It flows from us to the audience. They send it back to us, and we take it and send it back to them. Now it has more power and it keeps on building, like a circle of love. When they're really ready for us and that flow gets going, it's like heaven to us. It's delicious. Mmmmm! Mmmmm! Mmmmm!"

The Sound of Silence

"But few will hear the secrets
hidden within the notes."
—*Rumi*

Inside the world of audible sound—the vibrations we produce by blowing a flute, plucking the string of a harp, or by chanting—there is a secret world of sound. It is the sound that has always been and always will be, the essential sound, the intrinsic vibration of the universe. It is the sound of creation, the voice of God heard by Muhammad in the cave of Ghar-e-Hita, by Shiva in his Himalayan abode, and by Jesus in the wilderness. Called *anahat nad* in Sanskrit, *sarmad* by the Sufis, and the *logos* by some Christians, mystics of all traditions pray, meditate, fast, ingest sacred herbs, dance, and chant in their longing to hear the sound that transcends sound.

Just as our fascination with the delights of the material world may distract us from the world of Spirit, our absorption with the denser vibrations of audible sound makes it hard for us to hear the more subtle inner sounds. To listen to the inner music, we need silence. Christian medieval mystic Saint John of the Cross writes, "The Father uttered one word, that word is His Son, and He utters Him forever in everlasting silence; and in silence the soul has to hear it."

Chant is a pathway from manifest sound to the soundless sound, or in the words of Sufi teacher Allaudin Mathieu, "The bridge between sound and silence." Allaudin offers us some simple instructions for stepping onto that bridge. "Put the mantram on the breath and repeat it silently. You hear it, and feel it inside, but you don't audibly sound it. You're making sound . . . and you're not making sound. It's the sound of silence."

Chanting brings audible sound into such a refined state, it's as if a window were opened into the world of the inner, spiritual sound. Elias Amidon says, "Certainly the chant is important, but often it is the silence afterward that truly moves us. Sometimes after a *zhikr,* my teacher would have us just sit—thirty, forty-five minutes, just in that atmosphere that had been opened up, in the intimate sweetness." If we suddenly stop in the middle of a busy day and listen, we usually will hear a hustle-bustle of worldly sounds and the noise of our own thoughts and feelings. But according to author and Benedictine monk David Stendl-Rast, "When chant music stops . . . an audible silence reverberates through the room. . . . the silence is not merely sound's absence, but a mysterious presence, the immense nothingness that is our origin and our home. If we listen carefully, we discover that when all is said and done, chant inducts us into this silence that is the ground of our being."

> "Listen far beyond hearing,
> And call the unheard."
> —*Lao Tzu*

In this next story, Rabbi Tirzah Firestone tells of a journey with her congregation, a voyage through chant into the inner music of silence. Reb Tirzah relates, "According to Kabbalistic tradition, in the act of Creation the numinous light of God poured forth into vessels that were meant to receive His creative force. But the vessels couldn't contain the awesomeness of God's light and shattered, and the world is made up of their shards. Our job as evolving souls is to find and reclaim the hidden light.

"Gathered on the eve of Yom Kippur, the holiest day of the Jewish year, we prayed together to have this hidden light revealed:

'Ohr zarua la'Tzaddik
U-l'yish'ray layv simcha.'
'A light is sown for those who are pure in heart
And joy is hidden for the people who hold to the path.'
—*Psalm 97*

"To the accompaniment of light guitar and a gentle drumbeat, we slowly chanted, very aware that Jews all over the world were chanting with us: 'Ohr zarua la'Tzaddik . . .' We droned ever so slowly, allowing each syllable, each word to resonate. Completing the sacred phrase, we began a second round, the actual vibrations of sound invoking the Divine presence. And a third, 'A light is sown . . .' There was a feeling of awe, as if with each of the seven repetitions we were stripping away outer illusion, unmasking the appearances of reality to reveal the essential light of God.'

" 'Ohr zarua la'Tzaddik . . .' Through our chanting and prayer, we were also baring ourselves, stripping away our own outer appearances, our smaller selves, to let the light of our true nature shine forth. We intoned the fifth and sixth repetitions: 'Ohr zarua la'Tzaddik.' Waves of sound and energy moved through the room, pulsing in my body like a silent heartbeat. And for the seventh and final time, 'Ohr zarua la'Tzaddik . . . U-l'yish'ray layv simcha . . .'

"The silence in the room was deep. We had all stepped out of time and left this reality to enter another, one filled with the living presence of the souls of our ancestors, and the souls of our offspring not yet born. I am usually so driven, with so many chal-

lenges to face, my own struggles and those of the Jewish people.
. . . There was none of that here, none of the striving or grasping. Just peace—and the soulful, timeless pulsing of God's silent
music."

"If you want the truth, I'll tell you the truth,
   Listen to the secret sound, the real sound, which is inside you . . .
   The music from the strings no one touches."

—*Kabir*

Praise and Gratefulness

There is a story about another rabbi and the president of the temple
who are praying before the Holiest of Holies. The rabbi, overcome
with feelings of unworthiness before God, falls to his knees and
begins to intone, "Oh God, I'm a nobody. I'm a nobody." The
president, moved by this display of humility, also falls to his knees
and begins to pray, "Oh God, I'm a nobody. I'm a nobody." The
janitor, quietly sweeping in the back, is so moved seeing the leaders
of the congregation on their knees that he joins in too: "Oh God,
I'm a nobody. I'm a nobody." The president, upon seeing this, turns
to the rabbi with a raised eyebrow. Gesturing with his head toward
the janitor, he says, "So—look who thinks he's a nobody."

One of the greatest dangers on the spiritual path is what Buddhist
teacher Trungpa Rimpoche calls "spiritual materialism"—what results when our ego hijacks and co-opts our spiritual practice to serve
its own needs. "God speaks to *me* (and not to you) . . . Not my
will but Thine (and *I* know what God's will is) . . . *I* had the most
incredible experience chanting yesterday (probably an early sign of
incipient enlightenment)." We confuse self with Self. While all mys-

tical traditions tell us that God is inside, we need to remember to keep ourselves and the Divine in proper perspective. God is really, really big—and we're smaller than a grain of sand on an endless beach.

One of the things that can help keep us clear is the practice of chanting praise and gratefulness. It's not that God is so in need of positive feedback. "Praise" derives from the Latin *pretium,* meaning "reward or prize," and chanting praise is its own reward. We chant in honor of the Divine because it opens our heart and draws closer to us the presence of Spirit. As writer and theologian C. S. Lewis puts it, "Prayer doesn't change God, it changes me." When we chant to the Creator, we remember that it is not we who move heaven and earth. What a relief!

As long as there has been language, people have been intoning praise to Divine beings. The earliest identified historical author, Enheduanna, wrote this hymn to the Goddess Inanna in cuneiform tablets over five thousand years ago in ancient Sumeria:

"To my Lady enfolded in beauty.
Praise to Inanna."

From the dawn of history in India, the Upanishads chant God's praises: "All this universe is in the glory of God, of Shiva the God of love." Hieroglyphics carved in the stone of ancient Egypt proclaim: "God is One and Alone, and there is no other beside Him." For well over a thousand years, five times a day Muslims all over the world have prostrated themselves on their prayer mats facing in the direction of Mecca and intoned: "God is great. *Allah hu akbar.* God is great. I testify that there is none worthy of worship except God." The Psalms of the Old Testament, originally intoned by David,

are a beautiful and enduring honoring of God, punctuated by Hallelujah—"praise the Lord."

> "Shout unto the Lord, all the earth,
> Break forth and sing for joy, yea sing praises.
> Sing praises unto the Lord with the harp . . . Hallelujah!
> O Lord my God, Thou art very great . . . Hallelujah!
> I will sing praise to my Lord while I have any being . . .
> Hallelujah!"

In fact, if we peel away the linguistic nuances, the rough translation of most chants boils down to "Yea God!"

It is not just the Creator that we honor, but creation itself. Everywhere we turn, we are greeted by the loveliness and wonder of the
countless forms in which Spirit is cloaked. We need not search deep
in meditation for some invisible and formless presence, for the glory
of God is a gift for the senses: beauty for the eyes to behold, harmony for the ears, fragrance for the nose, ambrosia for the palate.
Every spiritual tradition intones in honor of creation:

> "Gaia, mother of all, splendid as rock,
> Eldest of all beings; I sing the greatness of Earth."
> —Greece, sixth century B.C.E.

From the Ashanti of West Africa:

> "O God, creator of our land,
> our earth, the trees, the animals and humans;
> All is for your honor."

The famous canticle of Saint Francis of Assisi has been chanted for half a millennium, from hymns sung in cathedrals and churches, to folk songs of medieval Italian troubadours and contemporary pop stars:

> "Be praised my Lord, for all Your creations
> And especially for Brother Sun
> who makes the day bright and luminous."

The Maori of New Zealand intone their traditional *karakia* chants—praises to *Io,* the "Heavenly One," at the breathtaking speed of three hundred syllables per minute. In this chant, they are praising the Spirit of the forests for sacrificing one of his "children" (the trees) for use by the tribe:

> "Kua kotia nga putake o te rakau o te whare nei."

As we give praise, we are reminded that this body, this life, and everything in it is a gift from Spirit.

> "O Great Spirit
> Whose voice I hear in the winds
> and whose breath gives life to all the world . . ."
> —*Native American chant*

In a world where technology provides the illusion of control over nature, where tomatoes appear to grow in cellophane packages in supermarket aisles and babies can be conceived in test-tubes, we sometimes forget that this is all a miracle of Spirit. When most of us are faced with questions like which dish to make for dinner or what color sweater to buy, rather than having enough to eat or even clothes to wear, it is all too easy to take the gifts of Spirit for granted.

Chanting our praise and gratitude reminds us of the preciousness of life. We greet the sun knowing that our life depends on its comings and goings:

> "Listen to the salutation to the dawn,
> Look to this day for it is life, the very life of life . . ."
> —*Sanskrit chant*

We savor each morsel of our food as though it were all we had:

> "We give thanks to the corn and her sisters,
> The beans and squashes, which give us life."
> —*Iroquois chant*

We hug our loved ones good night, knowing that any day we may be called apart:

> "You have given me your riches,
> I love you so."
> —*Contemporary popular chant*

Chant praises when you awake and when you lie down, when you come and when you go. Chant gratitude in health and in sickness, in times of scarcity and times of abundance. Honor Spirit which brings us life—in this very next breath.

> "Praise to the Breath of Life . . .
> Do not forsake me."
> —*Atharva Veda*

Hallelujah! Praise God! *Alhamdulillah! Jai Ram!*

Oneness

Surya Das, an American-born lama and lineage holder in the Dzogchen Tibetan Buddhist tradition, told me this powerful story of an experience with chant that occurred near the beginning of his training:

"It was my first trip to the East in 1971, and after some searching, I had met my teacher—a Buddhist lama in a hilltop monastery just outside Kathmandu (Nepal). I wanted very much to do a solo retreat, and the lama obliged by sending me up to a hut with the instructions to chant and listen to the sound of the waterfall. He taught me the famous one-hundred-syllable mantra of Vajra Satva—the Diamond Being, designed to vibrate in all the hundred states of consciousness. Devout Tibetan Buddhists are expected to chant this mantra 100,000 times over the course of their lives.

"I had just turned twenty-one and was eager to get started. My few belongings in my backpack, I hiked up to a place called Tatapani (meaning hot water). Settling into my tiny mud hut with its wood and thatched roof, I chanted and chanted, broken only by occasional light meals of *tsampa* (Tibetan barley flour) and tea. I was trying for four to five thousand repetitions per day—about twelve hours' worth. I sat by the waterfall, day after day, chanting my brains out. I don't know how many days I had been chanting when I first had this vision of my becoming a beautiful crystal chalice that was being filled up with pure light. There was so much energy that I stayed up all night chanting.

'Om Vajra Sattva Samaya: Manu Palaya:
Vajra Sattva: Tveno Patisha.'

"As the hours passed, I experienced becoming more and more transparent. Thoughts and perceptions began to float across the clear screen of my awareness as if in slow motion. It was as if the crystal chalice were beginning to fill up with nectar.

"The sound of the mantra and the sound of the waterfall became one sound. I no longer knew whether it was I or the waterfall that was chanting the mantra, whether I was chanting the waterfall, or the waterfall was chanting me. I suppose my lips were still moving, but it was truly the Self that was chanting.

"Every moment seemed like the eternal now—neither long nor short—out of time. I was becoming clear, like the sky, like the sun and beyond the sun, becoming a diamond light being—luminous consciousness. All my five senses folded in toward the center like an umbrella, withdrawing from this world as through the eye of a needle. . . . I became empty awareness. It was all the *Vajra Sattva,* the diamond being, reflections of a field of infinite Buddhas. It was me, and not me. I was them. It was . . .

"And at a certain point, like all experiences, it was over. The umbrella opened—empty awareness folded out back into the five senses, and I was in my body again . . . sitting by the hot springs . . . back in Nepal . . . purified."

Surya Das experienced oneness with the Divine through the practice of chant. The everyday sense of being "me" dissolved, like Rumi's "pieces of cloud . . . in sunlight"; like a cube of sugar in a cup of warm tea. It is the ineffable experience mystics have tried to describe as self giving way to the Self, of lover merging with the Beloved, of radiant light or universal sound—of becoming one with God. While Surya's account with its five thousand repetitions of a sacred mantra and diamond light beings may seem exotic, you don't have to travel to the Himalayas to find oneness with God.

Seventy-nine years of age, Katherine sits quietly in her chair by the window in her Ohio apartment, eyes closed and pure bliss on her face. A votive candle flickers on a card table holding small statues of Jesus, Joseph, and Mary. A bouquet of delicate blue flowers has been carefully placed next to the figure of the Virgin. The well-worn rosary beads move quickly through her tiny old hands as she chants softly to herself. The tones are just on the edge of her breath. If you walked into the room you would hear a melodic murmur, over and over:

"Hail Mary, full of grace, the Lord is with thee,
Blessed art thou amongst women and
Blessed is the fruit of thy womb, Jesus.
Hail Mary . . . Hail Mary . . . Hail Mary . . ."

Before evening casts its long shadow across her room, Katherine will have chanted her rosary more than a hundred times. "When I'm lost in the sounds of my prayer," she says, "I can feel myself melting into Jesus, and I'm the one being held in the arms of the Blessed Mother."

On the spiritual path, we don't have to travel far because we are already at our destination. God is always present. We *are* one with Spirit—whether we are in a moment of remembering, or lost in the trance of everyday life. As Elias Amidon likes to say, "The veils aren't around God; the veils are around us."

We are like a radio receiver that can be tuned to different bandwidths or stations. The energy of God is transmitting at its radiant frequency, every moment of our lives. Most of the time, we're simply tuned to other stations—we don't feel it. Those of us on a spiritual path are scanning the spectrum of our consciousness, looking for the right wavelength. From time to time, the signal comes in, but there's often static, so we try adjusting the tuning dial back and forth.

This is the nature of spiritual practice — a process of tuning ourselves, clearing away the static so that we become better receivers for Divine energy. Chanting, as we have seen, is a powerful means of aligning our bodies, hearts, and minds to the wavelength of Spirit. Our restless minds find peace in the repeating, rhythmic vibrations of chant. Our wandering hearts find a home in devotion to the Source of all love. And the anxiety of our grasping ego is channeled into praise and gratitude to the Creator.

As our being begins to resonate with the frequency of Spirit, we will sometimes have the experience of oneness with God, as seen in this story told to me by my longtime friend Prajna Hallstrom:

"The four of us walked into the meadow behind the retreat center carrying shovels, rice dyed yellow and red, a few crystals, and some silver dollars I picked up at the bank. Our task was to build a small shrine to the Goddess, and it was one of those perfect Colorado summer days, the sky so blue, the wind was blowing down off the ridge, and not another soul in sight.

"It was hot work in the noonday sun. John dug a hole while the rest of us gathered pale red sandstone rocks. We labored for several hours in silence. When it was complete, we looked down at the low stone wall enclosing the ceremonial fire pit. Raking the ground, I sprinkled the colored rice and buried the crystals and silver dollars.

"As if guided by some unspoken inner sense, without a word each of us went to sit on one of the four larger rocks marking the four directions. I suggested that we chant. Out of nowhere, I heard a strangely familiar melody and began to teach with great authority a chant that I had never heard before:

'Om Devi Ma.
Om Devi Ma.
Devi Devi Devi Devi.
Devi Ma Namah.'

"As we began chanting in Sanskrit 'I honor the Goddess Mother. I honor the Goddess Mother,' it was as if we were each holding a direction for the Goddess. The chant spiraled and grew in power. I felt as if a fountain of energy was generating in my navel and moving up through my heart and into my forehead. We chanted and chanted—there was no longer a sense of time. Only this incredible energy and the presence of the Goddess. But it was more than feeling Her presence. I was the Spirit of compassion. I was Her fierce and loving countenance. I was one with the Goddess."

While chanting, like all spiritual practice, requires intention, the experience of oneness with Spirit comes by grace, not directly as a result of our effort. The farmer tills the soil, plants the seeds, and waters the tender shoots, creating all the conditions most conducive to the miracle of life. Our spiritual practice, our chanting, our prayers, our meditation, our solitude, can create a welcome home for Spirit to enter our heart. But the power that grows the seeds and opens our hearts with its love is not ours to command. Should the Guest honor the home of our heart with His presence, it is always a blessing, always a gift. In our last story, we hear from a wilderness teacher named David LaChapelle how many years ago spontaneous toning brought the gift of Spirit into his young life:

"Long before I ever heard of chanting, when I was eight years old, we lived in Olympic National Park, where my father worked at a research station. I will always be grateful to my parents for having the wisdom and courage to let me wander freely in this magical world of mountains and glaciers. There is nothing like the sounds of water moving through that landscape—waterfalls, water flowing under the glacier, trickles of melting snow, all blending into a continuous sound like the roar of an ocean surf. The most remarkable thing is how the quality of sound changes as shifting winds change the temperature and air density. Tones modulate, becoming deeper and louder, then thinner and muted.

"Wandering over rocks and snow, listening to this symphony of sound, I would just begin singing. I would sing anything—made-up words, tones, I don't know what—but I would sing and sing and sing—for hours. Then I'd sit and stop singing and just listen—letting the many-textured sounds of water wash over me, always modulating, continuous, always changing, pulsing with life. My body somehow felt much larger than my physical body. Glacial downdrafts can be cold, but I was warmed from inside. Time stood still.

"These were the most peaceful moments I've ever experienced. Something happened there that has been unmatched in the many 'spiritual' experiences I've had since. It was my private world. I never spoke of it to a soul until many years later, but it placed an indelible stamp on me and my life. It was the innocence, the lack of any effort or artifice. . . . It was a gift from life."

Chant and sacred sound are gifts of Spirit. To lie alone under the stars and chant with the night wind. To send our children to sleep held in a tender song. To join with our community in a house of worship and intone a communal prayer. To sit with friends in the living room and chant for the sheer fun of it. Writing this book has been a wonderful opportunity for me to experience anew how much joy I have received from chanting. I am grateful that this music that I so love to create also brings such goodness to others.

To close our journey of discovering Spirit in sound, let us end with a chant. Imagine we are standing together in a large circle— you, me, and all those who are reading this book. Reach out in your imagination as if we were joining hands, and for this one moment, experience that you are connected to a host of other beings, like yourself, who seek love and Spirit through sound. And we join our voices to chant this closing prayer:

"May the blessings of God rest upon you.
May God's peace abide with you.
May God's presence illuminate your heart.
Now and forever more.

May your life be filled with the beauty and joy of chant.
May you share in a communion of voices and
hearts with those you love.
May your soul draw nourishment from the
deep well of sacred sound.
May your Spirit soar to heaven on wings of song."

Resource Guide

Section I: Bringing Chant into Your Home

CHANT: SPIRIT IN SOUND
The Best of World Chant
created by Robert Gass

Two volume set:
Disc one   *Ecstasy: The Fire of Devotion*
Disc two   *Stillness: The Journey Within*

I have created a companion recording to this book entitled *Chant: Spirit in Sound*. After reviewing hundreds of chant recordings, I selected my favorite traditional and contemporary chants from around the world (many of which are referred to in this book). This two volume set showcases the power and beauty of chant, allowing the listeners to enrich their homes, cars, and workplaces with sacred sound.

THE SPIRIT OF CHANT
The Best of Robert Gass & On Wings of Song

Spring Hill Music is celebrating the publishing of this book with a "best of" album drawn from my over fifteen CDs and tapes of chant and healing music. The forty-five voices of the renowned vocal group On Wings of Song perform my arrangements of best-loved chants from Hindu, Christian, Buddhist, Sufi,

Goddess, and Native American traditions. *The Spirit of Chant* includes a version of our well-known recording of *Om Namaha Shivaya*, an uplifting arrangement of the *Alleluia to the Pachelbel Canon in D*, and a deeply-meditative peformance of the Buddhist chant, *Heart of Perfect Wisdom*.

To order either of these two recordings, (or to obtain information on workshops with Robert and Judith Gass) contact:

Spring Hill Music
Box 800, Boulder, CO 80304
1-800-427-7680
Please send for a free catalog.

Spring Hill Music also carries the many recordings of chant I have made with On Wings of Song. Most of these are designed for you to be able to sing along:

- *Om Namaha Shivaya*
- *Alleluia*
- *Gloria*
- *O Great Spirit*
- *A Sufi Song of Love*
- *Kyrie*
- *From the Goddess*
- *Heart of Perfect Wisdom*
- *Shri Ram*
- *Ancient Mother*
- *Many Blessings*
- *Hara Hara Gurudeva*
- *Medicine Wheel*
- *Songs of Healing*

Here is a list of my favorite recordings of chant from all the traditions that we have explored:

Hindu Chant

Ravi Shankar; *Chants of India;* Angel Records.
    A splendid collection of traditional Sanskrit chants. Produced

by George Harrison, the album is both highly musical and imbued with devotional feeling. Includes the Gaayatri mantra described in chapter 4.

Krishna Das; *Pilgrim Heart;* Triloka Records.
These somewhat westernized versions of traditional Sanskrit chants have a lot of heart and are great for singing along. I really enjoy this album.

Swami Chidvilasananda; *Om Namo Bhagavate Muktananadaya;* SYDA Foundation.
Sixty minutes of one devotional chant, slowly building to an ecstatic climax. Recorded live with thousands of chanters in traditional call and response with the guru of the Siddha yoga lineage. Good for singing along.

Sri Laxmi Narayan Tiwari; *From the Circle of Saints;* Yoga Int. Books & Tapes.
For those who prefer a more traditional, less westernized recording, this album contains six Sanskrit chants sung in call and response with a North Indian chant master.

Christian Chant

Monastic Choir of St. Peter's Abbey; *Gregorian Sampler;* Paraclete Music.
A lovely anthology of Gregorian chant from the Benedictine Monastery in Solesmes, France.

Gothic Voices; *A Feather on the Breath of God;* Hyperion Records.
Grammy Award–winning recording of chants by the twelfth-century mystic Abbess Hildegard of Bingen.

Soeur Marie Keyrouz; *Chant Byzantin—Passion et Resurrection;* Harmonia Mundi.

Haunting Greek and Arabic chants from the Eastern Orthodox Church tradition. Performed by an internationally renowned Lebanese nun and monastic choir.

African Chant

Monks of Keur Moussa; *Sacred Chant & African Rhythms from Senegal;* Sounds True.
  Performing on traditional African instruments, the monks joyfully wed Western liturgical chant with tribal rhythms and song.

Misc. artists; *African Voices;* Narada.
  A wonderful collection of songs by five African artists. Contemporary yet rooted in their rich musical and spiritual traditions.

Misc. artists; *Afro-Cuba: A Musical Anthology;* Rounder Records.
  Sacred chant from the Yoruba, Arara, and Lucumi traditions. Completely authentic, including field recordings of rituals and Orisha invocations.

Buddhist Chant

Monks of Sera Je Monastery; *Tibet;* Amiata Records.
  The chanting of Tibetan monks (including overtone chant) in traditional ceremonies recorded in Dharamsala, India. Accompanied by an informative and beautifully illustrated booklet about Tibetan Buddhism.

Lama Gyurme & Jean-Philippe Rykiel; *The Lama's Chant;* Sony Music.
  A Tibetan lama chanting traditional prayers with tasteful synthesizer accompaniment. Well-produced and heartful.

Thich Nhat Hanh & Sister Chan Khong; *Drops of Emptiness;* Sounds True.

Chants, prayers, and sung poems of Vietnamese Zen priest and author Thich Nhat Hanh from his spiritual community of Plum Village in France.

Sufi/Islamic Chant

Oruc Guvenc & Tumata; *Ocean of Remembrance;* Interworld Records.
 Turkish Sufi shaykh and small ensemble performing *zhikrs* (repetitive chants) and improvisations. Well-produced, good energy, and very accessible to western listeners.

Chant des Derviches de Turquie; Arion Records (France).
 An actual *zhikr* ceremony of the Halveti Brotherhood of Turkish Sufis as described in Chapter 4, capturing the intensity of a roomful of chanting dervishes.

Misc. artists; *The Music of Islam;* Celestial Harmonies.
 Anthology of Islamic sacred music, including Qur'an chanting, drum chants from Nubia, vocal ragas from India, and chant from Yemen and Morocco.

Nusrat Fateh Ali Khan; *Shahen-Shah;* Realword.
 An ecstatic recording from the famous master of Sufi Qawwali music of Pakistan. Passionate and devotional high-energy chant.

Native American Chant

Misc. artists; *Tribal Voices;* Earthbeat Records.
 A very good collection of fourteen intertribal contemporary and traditional chants and songs. Well-produced with a lot of variety.

Joanne Shenandoah & Lawrence Laughing; *Orenda;* Silver Wave.
 Beautiful and melodic traditional chants of the Six Nations

Iroquois. Performed and produced in a style very pleasing to contemporary ears.

Misc. artists; *Traditional Voices;* Canyon Records.
An extensive collection of field recordings of authentic traditional Native American chants, recorded in the fifties and sixties at ceremonies, dances, and powwows.

Misc. Chant

Chorale Mystique; *Chants Mystiques: Hidden Treasures of a Living Tradition;* Polygram.
The best album I have heard of Jewish chant. Drawn from both western and Oriental Jewish traditions, the chants are exquisitely performed by world-renowned cantor Alberto Mizrahi and choir.

Misc. artists; *Voices of Forgotten Worlds;* Ellipsis Arts.
A double CD collection of chants and songs from indigenous cultures recorded on location. Includes an excellent ninety-page booklet with color photographs about the culture and music of traditional peoples.

Sainkho; *Naked Spirit;* Amiata Records.
Wonderful contemporary arrangements of traditional Siberian chant and song. Proficient in Tuvan overtone singing, Sainkho also plays mouth harp and shaman's drum.

Libana; *The Circle Is Cast;* Spinning Records.
A collection of circle and ritual chants celebrating women's traditions and Goddess spirituality. Many of the selections are good for singing along.

Singh Kaur and Kim Robertson; *Crimson Collection Vol. I & II;* Invincible Productions.

Two extended Sanskrit chants from the Sikh tradition. Singh Kaur's lovely and pure voice is accompanied by Celtic harp. Good for singing along or to create a gentle ambiance.

Modern Chant

Tulku; *Season of Souls;* Triloka.
A creative and highly musical combination of chant from different traditions set to contemporary rhythm grooves.

David Hykes and the Harmonic Choir; *Hearing Solar Winds;* Harmonia Mundi.
An extraordinary and magical demonstration of overtone chanting from this contemporary master of harmonics.

Jonathan Goldman; *Chakra Chants;* Etherean Music.
Healing music designed to activate the chakras by the founder of The Sound Healers Association.

Sheila Chandra; *Weaving My Ancestors' Voices;* Real World Records.
This talented Indian-born singer chants, tones, and vocalizes her way through a stunning album of haunting solo voice, weaving Indian, Celtic, Islamic, Gregorian, and Iberian tonalities.

You can order any of these titles from Spring Hill Music. Ask for their catalog of chant recordings.

Other Recorded Resources

For a wide selection of audio courses, CDs, and audiotapes, send for a catalog from:

Sounds True
P.O. Box 8010, Boulder, CO 80306 1 (800) 333-9185

In particular, I recommend:

Bourgeault, Rev. Cynthia, *Singing the Psalms*
Campbell, Don, *Healing Yourself with Your Own Voice*
Gardner, Kay, *Music as Medicine*
Kabir, Chaitanya, *Divine Singing*
Newham, Paul, *The Singing Cure*

Jeff Volk (video: *Of Sound, Mind & Body)*
    available from: MACROmedia
    219 Grant Road, Newmarket, NH 03857 (603) 659-2929

Sacred Spirit Music (mail order catalog of sacred music)
    5 Abode Rd., New Lebanon, NY 12125 (518) 794-7860

Section II: How to Find Live Chant in Your Area

Recorded chant is great, but for those of you who want to experience
the vital, breathing energy of live chanting in groups, you may need
to embark on a quest.

In my hometown of Boulder, Colorado, where one in every three
people seems to be a body worker, health food is the municipal diet,
and there are four stores selling crystals on the downtown mall, one
does not have to be a professional sleuth to track down chanting. In
many places, however, your search may be more challenging. I tried
checking in that atlas for modern explorers—the Yellow Pages—but
found that the listings skipped from "Chambers of Commerce" to
"Charities"—no "Chant."

Depending on where you live, finding live chant may be an easy
or arduous journey. But pilgrimage has a long tradition in spiritual

practice, and the destination—chanting—is worth the trip. Here are some travel trips:

1. Ask local ministers, priests, or rabbis for their recommendations for participating in live chant in your area. A call to a Catholic church might yield leads of where to go hear Gregorian chant. Ask ministers about opportunities for chanting psalmody. If you hear of any Taizé services anywhere near you, *make sure to go.* This is some of the most alive, participatory chanting anywhere. Jewish Renewal services are always brimming with sing-alongs and chant.

2. If you are fortunate enough to have Dances of Universal Peace in your area, they provide wonderful evenings of sacred dance and chant from all traditions. See their listing in section III of the resource guide.

3. There are several national organizations through which you may be able to participate in Sanskrit devotional chanting. Try contacting the Mata Amritanandamayi Center which books regular tours of the United States and Europe for their guru Ammachi; or the headquarters of SYDA yoga in South Fallsburg, New York, to see if there is a local group in your area. Contact information for both is in section III of the resource guide.

4. Many regions have newspapers for those interested in spirituality, obtainable at health food stores and metaphysical bookstores. Look through their listings for ashrams, yoga centers, retreat centers, or other places that might offer chant. (The people who work at these places may also have ideas.)

5. Try the Yellow Pages in your telephone directory under "Meditation" or "Yoga." Make some calls and ask about chanting.

6. Native American art galleries may know about powwows where non-Indians are welcome to enjoy the great drumming, dancing, and chant.
7. In recent years, groups ranging from Tibetan monks to Sufi Qawwali singers have brought some of the world's most exotic chant on tour to the West.
8. Travel further afield. Check out courses on chanting at places like Omega in Rhinebeck, New York (800) 944-1001, and Kripalu in Lenox, Massachusettes (800) 741-7353.

Good luck on your journey. May it lead you to a room filled with the sacred vibrations of chant.

Section III: Workshops and Other Resources

Here's how to reach some of the healers, teachers, and chant leaders whose work is discussed in the book:

Ammachi (Hindu devotional chanting)
Mata Amritanandamayi Center
P.O. Box 613, San Ramon, CA 94583
(510) 537-9417 http://www.ammachi.org

Margo Anand (tantra workshops)
Skydancing Tantra International, Inc.
524 San Anselmo Ave., Suite 133, San Anselmo, CA 94960
(415) 456-7310 http://www.skydancing.com

George Brandon (workshops on African culture)
409 Edgecombe Ave. 4D, New York, NY 10032
(212) 368-8787 ogun@sci.ccny.cuny.edu

Brooke Medicine Eagle
(shamanism/Native American workshops)
#1 Second Avenue East, C401, Polson, MT 59860
(406) 883-4686 http://www.medicine-eagle.com

Don Campbell (*The Mozart Effect*; music and healing)
P.O. Box 4179, Boulder, CO 80306
(800) 721-2177 http://www.mozarteffect.com

Deepak Chopra (seminars; Ayurvedic healing)
The Chopra Center for Well-being
7630 Fay Ave., La Jolla, CA 92037
(888) 424-6772 http://www.chopra.com

Elizabeth Cogburn (ceremonialist; rituals)
P.O. Box 11, Arroyo Seco, NM 87514

Dances of Universal Peace (formerly "Sufi" dancing)
International Network for the Dances of Universal Peace
444 NE Ravenna Blvd., #306, Seattle, WA 98115
(206) 522-4353 http://www.DancesofUniversalPeace.org

Steven and Meredith Foster (wilderness rites of passage)
P.O. Box 55, Big Pine, CA 93513
lostbrdrs@telis.org

Kay Gardner (sound healing and Goddess chanting)
P.O. Box 33, Stonington, ME 04681
(207) 367-5552 evenkeel@hypernet.com

Judith Gass (seminars; ceremonialist; coaching and retreats)
895 Rainlily Lane, Boulder, CO 80304
jgass@indra.com

Jonathan Goldman (sound healing)
Healing Sounds Seminars/Spirit Music/

The Sound Healers Association
P.O. Box 2240, Boulder, CO 80306
(800) 246-9764 http://www.Healingsounds.com

David LaChapelle (wilderness rites of passage)
Box 21592, Juneau, AK 99802
dlachape@ptialaska.net

Oscar Miro-Quesada (shamanism workshops)
2006 N.W. 3rd Ave., Delray Beach, FL 33444
(561) 265-1445

Onye Onyemaechi (African chant workshops and tapes)
P.O. Box 1203, Rohnert Park, CA 94927
(707) 538-0421

Opening the Heart Workshops
379 Boston Post Road, #212
Sudbury, MA 01776
openhart@acunet.net

Molly Scott (Sound and Music healing)
Creative Resonance Institute
Box U, Charlemont, MA 01339
(413) 339-5501

Lama Surya Das (Dzogchen Buddhism)
The Dzogchen Foundation
P.O. Box 734, Cambridge, MA 02140
(617) 628-1702 http://www.dzogchen.org

SYDA Foundation (Hindu/yoga chanting)
371 Brickman Road, P.O. Box 600, South Fallsburg, NY 12779
(914) 434-2000 http://www.siddhayoga.org

Luisah Teish (Yoruba ceremonialist; seminars)
2930 Shattuck Ave., #28, Berkeley, CA 94705

Karolyn van Putten (toning)
3516 Mirasol Avenue, Oakland, CA 94605
(510) 562-2433 tonesinger@aol.com

Zen Peacemaker Order
1400A Cerro Gordo Rd., Sante Fe, NM 97501
(505) 983-5541 http://www.zpo.org

Section IV: Written Resources

Berendt, Joachim-Ernst, *Nada Brahma: The World is Sound* (Rochester, VT: Destiny, 1987). The leading book on the mysticism of sound.

Campbell, Don, *The Roar of Silence* (Wheaton, Ill.: Quest Books, 1989). A practical guide to toning.

Campbell, Don, *The Mozart Effect* (New York: Avon Books, 1997). The best general book on the power of music on healing and consciousness.

Gardner, Kay, *Sounding the Inner Landscape* (Rockport, Mass.: Element, 1990). A good overview of music and healing.

Goldman, Jonathan, *Healing Sounds: The Power of Harmonics* (Boston: Element, 1996). Good introduction to harmonics and healing.

Jourdain, Robert, *Music, the Brain, and Ecstasy* (New York: Avon Books, 1997). Popular book on the physiology of music.

Keyes, Laurel Elizabeth, *Toning: The Creative Power of the Voice* (Marina del Rey, CA: De Vorss, 1973). The pioneering work on toning.

Khan, Hazrat Inayat, *The Mysticism of Sound and Music* (Boston: Shambhala, 1996). Sufi master on the mysticism of sound.

Kittleson, Mary Lynn, *Sounding the Soul* (Einsiedeln, Switzerland: Daimon, 1996). Jungian view on the power of music.

Leeds, Joshua, *Sonic Alchemy* (Sausalito, Calif.: InnerSong Press, 1997). Good anthology of articles on sound, healing, and chant.

LeMee, Katherine, *Chant: The Origins, Form, Practice, and Healing Power of Gregorian Chant* (New York: Bell Tower, 1994). The best popular book on Gregorian chant.

Mathieu, W. A. *The Musical Life* (Boston: Shambhala, 1994). Interesting series of essays on music, consciousness, and life.

Newham, Paul, *The Singing Cure: An Introduction to Voice Movement Therapy* (Boston: Shambhala, 1994). Good overview on the psychology and power of the voice.

Reck, David, *Music of the Whole Earth* (New York: Charles Scribner's Sons, 1977). The best book on ethnic music from around the world.

Tomatis, Alfred, *The Ear and Language* (Ontario, Canada: Moulin Publishing, 1996). Overview of his pioneering work on sound and healing.

Section V: Music for Chanting

Here are the music and words to some of my favorite chants. I have included the chords for those that can be accompanied by guitar or piano. For those chants that I have recorded, there is also the name of the album on which they may be found. These chants are powerful tools for transformation. May they bring you blessings of joy and Spirit.

Christian Chants

Ubi Caritas
LATIN CHANT

"Where true love and charity are found, God Himself is there." This Latin chant is from the ecumenical Taizé worship community. The top line is the melody; the bottom a lovely harmony.

Kyrie

MUSIC BY ABRAHAM SUSSMAN & JONATHAN LIEFF

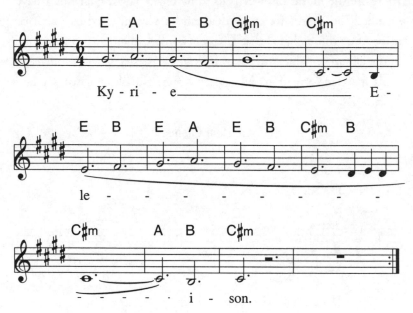

Sometimes sung during the Catholic Mass, the words *Kyrie Eleison* are actually Greek (though the rest of the mass used to be in Latin) and mean "God have mercy."

Can be found on the recording *Alleluia*.

Jubilate Deo

LATIN CHANT

This Latin chant (meaning "Praise God") is a delightful and relatively easy six-part round. The numbers above the staff indicate where the parts enter.

Can be found on the recording: *Many Blessings*.

Native American Chants

Earth Is Our Mother

E drone

1. The Earth— is our Mo - ther,— we must take
2. Her sac - red ground we walk up - on—with e - very

care of her, the Earth— is our Mo - ther,—
step we take, her sac - red ground we walk up - on—

_ we must take care of her.
_ with e - very step we take.

Hey— yan - a ho— yan - a hey— yan yan,
Hey— yan - a ho— yan - a hey— yan yan,

hey— yan - a ho— yan - a hey— yan yan.———
hey— yan - a ho— yan - a hey— yan yan.———

I like to chant this when walking. Also good with drum or shaker. Can be found on the recording *Humanity*.

The Infinite Sun
SIOUX CHANT

Let me be one with the in - fin - ite Sun for ev - er and ev - er and ev - er.

Kee - ay wah - tay len - ya len - ya mah - ho - tay,

hi - ah - no, hi - ah - no, hi - ah - no.

This chant is best accompanied by a simple drumbeat or rattle.

Woa Woa

ARAPAHO CHANT

Woa Woa is from the Arapaho tradition and is said to be the sound of the he-wolf calling to the she-wolf, and her answer. This is an excellent chant to do outdoors—the circular rhythms of the chant pulse harmoniously with natural rhythms.

Can be found on the recording *Medicine Wheel*.

Hindu Chants

Om Namaha Shivaya

This powerful and widely chanted Sanskrit mantra to Shiva can be translated as: "I honor the Divine within."

Can be found on the recording *Om Namaha Shivaya.*

Shri Ram

Shri— Ram Jai— Ram Jai— Jai——Ram— Om. Shri—

Ram Jai— Ram Jai— Jai——Ram— Om Shri—

Another popular Sanskrit chant using the seed syllable OM, this chant honors the Divine in the incarnation of Rama. It can be sung in traditional *kirtan* style, beginning slowly, then building up to an ecstatic climax.

Can be found on the recording *Shri Ram.*

Gopala

This Sanskrit chant honors the Divine in the incarnation of Krishna and sings of the love for the baby Krishna (called Gopala) by his mother (Devaki) and foster father (the cow-herder, Nanda). The chant is typically sung sweetly, almost as a lullaby.

Goddess/Earth Chants

Isis Astarte

BY CAITLIN MULLIN & DEENA METZGER

I - sis, As - tar - te, Di - an - a, Hec - a - te, De -

me - ter, Ka - li, I - nan - na.

This chanted recitation of names of the Goddess has been widely used in women's circles and rituals for many years. The chant is a powerful invocation and honoring of the feminine face of the Divine. It can be sung percussively, putting special emphasis on the consonants. It may also be chanted in a whisper. Another good chant for drum or rattle.

Can be found on the recording *From the Goddess*.

Ancient Mother

TRADITIONAL

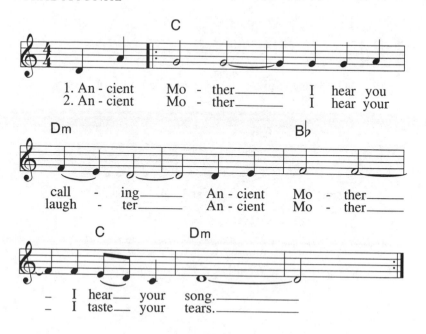

1. An - cient Mo - ther_____ I hear you
2. An - cient Mo - ther_____ I hear your

call - ing_____ An - cient Mo - ther_____
laugh - ter_____ An - cient Mo - ther_____

- I hear__ your song._____
- I taste__ your tears._____

This beautiful chant honors the Great Mother.
    Can be found on the recording *Ancient Mother.*

O Great Spirit

BY ADELE GETTY

O Great Spi - rit, earth, sun, sky and sea.

You are— in - side,—— and all a - round— me.

A perfect chant for communing with the natural elements.
Can be found on the recording *O Great Spirit.*

Mother Moon

TRADITIONAL

Mo-ther moon shine down on— me— I am you and

you are— me.— And we are part of e-very-thing,—

we are part of e - very - thing.

For special power, sing this chant outdoors at night looking up to
greet the moon.

Sufi Chant

Kalama
BY S.I.R.S PUBLICATIONS

La   i - la - ha.   El   A - llah hu.

llah hu. Mo - ham - med   ar - Ra - ssoul li -

llah, Mo - ham-med   ar - Ra - ssoul li - llah.

Kalama means the "Divine word." These lines are a central prayer in the Islamic faith, traditionally bearing witness that there is one God and that Muhammad is His Prophet. Non-Islamic Sufis sometimes reinterpret the second line as: "We each embody the Divine Message."

Jewish Chants

Niggun

TRADITIONAL

A classic wordless Chassidic niggun. Try using the syllables "dai" and "dee." This can be sung slowly, with the feeling pouring through the melody, or build it up into a foot-stomping "table banger."

Pitchu lee

HEBREW CHANT
MUSIC BY SHLOMO CARLEBACH

Written by the late Rabbi Shlomo Carlebach, this Hebrew chant translates as:

"Open for me the gates of righteousness.
I will enter them and thank God."

Return Again
MUSIC BY SHLOMO CARLEBACH

Re-turn a - gain. Re-turn a - gain.__ Re-

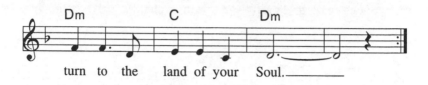

turn to the land of your Soul._____

Re-turn to who you are. Re-turn to what you are.

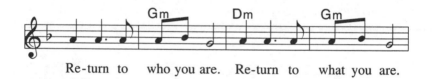

Re-turn to where you are. Born and re - born a - gain.

One of my all-time favorite chants, this is another well-known composition by Reb Shlomo.

Can be found on the recording *Songs of Healing.*

African Chant

Funga Alafia
TRADITIONAL NIGERIAN

Fun - ga a - la - fi - a, a - 'che,— a - 'che,

fun - ga— i - lay - ya, a - 'che,— a - 'che

Fung - ga a - la - fi - a, a - 'che,— a - 'che,

fun - ga— i - lay - ya, a - 'che,— a - 'che.

This traditional Nigerian greeting song means: "Welcome. May you have good health and be at peace with your neighbors. Power to you." It should be sung with a Spirited feel, can be done as a call and response, and like all West African chant, enjoys being accompanied by percussion.

Trans-denominational

Listen, Listen, Listen

BY PARAMAHANSA YOGANANDA

Lis-ten, lis-ten, lis - ten to my heart's song.

my heart's song. I will ne-ver for-get___you, I will

ne-ver for-sake___you. I will ne-ver for-sake___ you.___

Written by Yogananda, author of *Autobiography of a Yogi* and one of the early bringers of yoga to the West, this is one of the great devotional chants. Judith and I were married to this song, and it was one of the original chants of the Opening the Heart workshops.

Can be found on the recording *Songs of Healing.*

From Thee I Receive

BY JOSEPH & NATHAN SEGAL

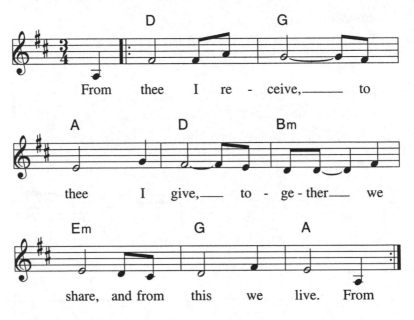

This melody metamorphisized from the original by singing Rabbis Joseph and Nathan Segal because I learned it from a tone-deaf man named Moshe in rural Maine. This wonderful chant has been our family's grace before meals for over twenty-five years.

Can be found on the recording *Many Blessings*.

May the Long Time Sun

TRADITIONAL

May the long time   sun shine up - on you,

all love sur - round___ you, and the pure

light with - in___ you   guide your way   home.

Another of the original healing chants from the Opening the Heart workshops, I learned this from the Cambridge Sufis in the early seventies and have been delighted to pass it on to so many others.

Can be found on the recording *Songs of Healing.*

Wherever You Go

BY GREGORY NORBERT, O.S.B. WESTON PRIORY

This text from the Book of Ruth was set to music by the Monks of Weston Priory, whose singing ministry has delighted Christians and non-Christians alike for decades. A wonderful chant for sharing love, healing, marriage.

Can be found on the recording *Songs of Healing.*

Go in Beauty
TRADITIONAL

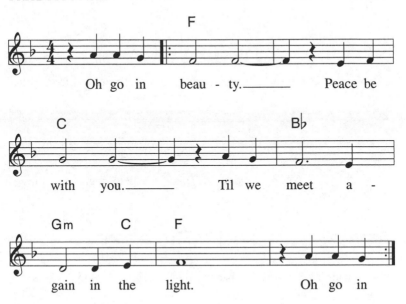

I learned this song from Rabbi David Zeller of Jerusalem, a beautiful minstrel of Spirit.

Can be found on the recording *Songs of Healing*.

Thank You for This Day
FROM THE NATIVE AMERICAN CHURCH

This Native American–inspired song is a "zipper song." In the phrase, "Thank you for this day," you can keep substituting words for "day" to fit the occasion: Thank you for this food . . . Thank you for these friends . . . Thank you for the sky . . . and so on.

May the Blessings of God
BY S.I.R.S. PUBLICATIONS

Good for rituals of leave-taking.

There is an excellent songbook of over four hundred additional chants called *Songs for Earthlings,* available from Emerald Earth Publishing, Box 4326, Philadelphia, PA 19118.

Bibliography

Babalula, S. A. *The Content and Form of Yoruba Chant.* Oxford: Clarendon Press, 1966.

Barks, Coleman (Trans.). *The Illuminated Rumi.* New York: Broadway Books, 1997.

Beaulieu, John. *Music and Sound in the Healing Arts.* Tarrytown, NY: Station Hill Press, 1987.

Bly, Robert. *The Soul Is Here for Its Own Joy.* Hopewell, NJ: Ecco Press, 1995.

Bunt, Leslie. *Music Therapy: An Art Beyond Words.* London: Routledge, 1994.

Campbell, Don (Ed.). *Music and Miracles.* Wheaton, IL: Quest Books, 1992.

Campbell, Don, *Music: Physician for Times to Come.* Wheaton, IL: Quest Books, 1991.

Cook, Pat Moffitt. *Shaman, Jhankri & Néle: Music Healers of Indigenous Cultures.* Rosyln, New York: Ellipsis Arts, 1997.

Curtis, Natalie. *The Indian's Book.* New York: Dover Publications, 1950.

Eliade, Mircea. *Shamanism: Archaic Techniques of Ecstasy.* Princeton, NJ: Princeton University Press, 1964.

Foster, Steven, and Meredith Little. *The Roaring of the Sacred River.* New York: Prentice Hall, 1989.

Frager, Robert. *Essential Sufism.* San Francisco: HarperSan Francisco, 1997.

Gandhi, Mahatma. *All Men Are Brothers.* New York: Continuum, 1980.

Gardner-Gordon. *The Healing Voice.* Freedom, CA: The Crossing Press, 1993.

Garfield, Leah Maggie. *Sound Medicine.* Berkeley, CA: Celestial Arts, 1987.

Griffiths, Bede. *Universal Wisdom.* New York: HarperCollins, 1994.

Halifax, Joan. *Shamanic Voices.* New York: Dutton, 1979.

Hamel, Peter Michael. *Through Music to the Self.* Rockport, MA: Element Books, 1984.

Harner, Michael. *The Way of the Shaman.* New York: Harper Row, 1980.

Harvey, Andrew. *The Essential Mystics.* San Francisco: HarperSan Francisco, 1996.

Hirschfield, Jane (Ed.). *Women in Praise of the Sacred.* New York: HarperCollins, 1994.

Idelson, A. Z. *Jewish Music in Its Historical Development.* New York: Henry Holt, 1929.

Jacobs, Alan. *The Element Book of Mystical Verse.* Rockport, MA: Element Books, 1997.

Kaku, Michio, and Jennifer Thompson. *Beyond Einstein.* New York: Doubleday, 1987.

Kapleau, Philip. *Zen: Dawn in the West.* Garden City, NY: Anchor Press/ Doubleday, 1979.

Lane, Deforia. *Music as Medicine.* Grand Rapids, MI: Zondervan Publishing, 1994.

Lipsker, Eli, and Velvel Pasternak. *Chabad Melodies.* Owings Mills, MD: Tara Publications, 1997.

Mathieu, W. A. *The Listening Book.* Boston: Shambhala, 1991.

McClellan, Randall. *The Healing Forces of Music.* Rockport, MA: Element Books, 1991.

Mitchell, Stephen. *The Enlightened Heart.* New York: Harper & Row, 1989.

Mosley, Ivo. *Earth Poems.* San Francisco: HarperSan Francisco, 1996.

Moyne, John, and Coleman Barks. *Open Secret: Versions of Rumi.* Putney, VT: Threshold Books, 1984.

Radha, Swami Sivananda. *Mantras: Words of Power.* Spokane, WA: Timeless Books, 1994.

Roberts, Elizabeth, and Elias Amidon. *Earth Prayers.* San Francisco: HarperSan Francisco, 1991.

Roberts, Elizabeth, and Elias Amidon. *Life Prayers.* San Francisco: HarperSan Francisco, 1996.

Rudhyar, Dane. *The Magic of Tone and the Art of Music.* Boston: Shambhala, 1982.

Savin, Olga (Trans.). *The Way of a Pilgrim.* Boston: Shambhala, 1991.

Schelling, Andrew. *For Love of the Dark One.* Boston: Shambhala, 1993.

Shankar, Ravi. *My Music, My Life.* New Delhi, India: Vikas Publishing House, 1968.

Shapiro, Rabbi Rami M. *Wisdom of the Jewish Sages.* New York: Bell Tower, 1993.

Sheldrake, Rupert. *The Presence of the Past.* Rochester, VT: Park Street Press, 1995.

Shiloah, Amnon. *Jewish Musical Traditions.* Detroit: Wayne State University Press, 1992.

Singh, Ranjie. *Self-Healing.* Ontario, Canada: Health Psychology Associates, 1996.

Star, Jonathan. *Rumi: In the Arms of the Beloved.* New York: Tarcher/ Putnam, 1997.

Stein, Diane. *A Women's Book of Ritual.* Freedom, Calif.: Crossing Press, 1990.

Steindl-Rast, David, with Sharon Lebell. *Music of Silence.* Berkeley, CA: Seastone Press, 1998.

Surya Das. *Awakening the Buddha Within.* New York: Broadway Books, 1997.

Teish, Luisah. *Jambalaya.* San Francisco: HarperSanFrancisco, 1985.

Telushkin, Rabbi Joseph. *Jewish Literature.* New York: Morrow, 1991.

About the Author

Robert Gass has been known for leading edge work in human consciousness, music, and healing for over twenty-five years. Holding a doctorate in Clinical Psychology and Public Practice from Harvard University, his work has synthesized the diverse areas of humanistic psychology, music, business, work with the terminally ill, political activism, and spiritual studies.

As an organizational consultant and healer, Robert has worked for senior executives at corporations such as Chase Manhattan, General Motors, and Pillsbury, as well as nonprofits such as Greenpeace, where he was acting board chair. He currently serves as a personal coach to well-known business, political, and spiritual leaders. He and his wife, Judith, are the creators of the highly regarded Opening the Heart workshops, and hundreds of thousands of people have participated in his seminars on spirituality, relationships, and leadership at universities, businesses, educational centers, and conferences around the world.

Also a highly regarded composer, performer, and recording artist with a career spanning classical music, rock, and chant, Robert has released over twenty albums of music to uplift the human spirit with his renowned choral group On Wings of Song. His recording of *Om Namaha Shivaya* was hailed by *New Age Journal* as "one of the most influential recordings of the last twenty years."

Robert lives in Boulder, Colorado, with his wife and three children.

Spring Hill Music is an independent record label founded by Robert Gass to produce music that uplifts the human spirit. Our catalog features recordings that may be of interest to readers of *Chanting: Discovering the Spirit in Sound.*

CHANT: SPIRIT IN SOUND
The Best of World Chant
   The two-volume companion recording to this book

THE SPIRIT OF CHANT
The best of Robert Gass/On Wings of Song
   A collection drawn from Robert's twenty albums of sacred music

THE MOZART EFFECT
Healing music compiled by Don Campbell, author of the
   bestselling book *The Mozart Effect*

The complete catalog of recordings by by Robert Gass/On
   Wings of Song

Thirty great recordings of sacred chant from all the world's
   traditions selected by Robert Gass

Please send for a free catalog:

Spring Hill Music
Box 800
Boulder, CO 80306
1 (800) 427-7680